This
Sporting
Life

Also edited by Emilie Buchwald
and Ruth Roston:

Mixed Voices: Contemporary Poems about Music

*The Poet Dreaming in the Artist's House:
Contemporary Poems about the Visual Arts*

This Sporting Life

Poems about Sports and Games

Edited by
Emilie Buchwald
and
Ruth Roston

MILKWEED
EDITIONS

Published 1998 by Milkweed Editions
Printed in the United States of America
Cover design by Don Leeper
Cover photo by Angela Raskob, Image Bank
Interior photographs by Beth Olson
Interior design by Randy Scholes
The text of this book is set in Bembo
98 99 00 01 02   5 4 3 2 1
Second Edition

Milkweed Editions is a not-for-profit publisher. Original publication of
this book was supported in part by a grant provided by the National
Endowment for the Arts, by the Metropolitan Regional Arts Council
from funds appropriated by the Minnesota State Legislature, and by the
United Arts Fund with special assistance from the McKnight Foundation.
This edition of the book was made possible in part by additional funds
from the Elmer L. and Eleanor J. Andersen Foundation; James Ford
Bell Foundation; Bush Foundation; Cray Research, a Silicon Graphics
Company; Dayton's, Mervyn's, and Target Stores by the Dayton Hudson
Foundation; Doherty, Rumble and Butler Foundation; Dorsey Whitney
Foundation; General Mills Foundation; Honeywell Foundation; Hubbard
Foundation; Jerome Foundation; The McKnight Foundation; Andrew
W. Mellon Foundation; Challenge and Creation and Presentation
Programs of the National Endowment for the Arts; Norwest Foundation
on behalf of Norwest Bank Minnesota, Norwest Investment
Management & Trust, Lowry Hill, Norwest Investment Services, Inc.;
Lawrence and Elizabeth Ann O'Shaughnessy Charitable Income Trust in
honor of Lawrence M. O'Shaughnessy; Oswald Family Foundation; Piper
Jaffray Companies, Inc.; Ritz Foundation; John and Beverly Rollwagen
Fund of the Minneapolis Foundation; The St. Paul Companies, Inc.;
James R. Thorpe Foundation; and by the support of generous individuals.

Library of Congress Catalog Number: 86–60749
ISBN 1–57131–404–0

This book is printed on acid-free paper.

"what I'm saying is
it's up to you"

—David Allan Evans, "THE BULL RIDER'S ADVICE"

Contents

PLAY BALL!

. . . Baseball

. . . Basketball

. . . Football

ON INCANDESCENT FEET: Running, Jogging, Skating, Skiing

PURSUIT: Hunting, Fishing, Boxing, Wrestling

COACHES

PLAYING THE GAME

THIS SPORTING LIFE

EDITORS' PREFACE

"Έρδοι τις, ἤν ἔκαστος εἰδειη τέχνην."
ARISTOPHANES.

"Let each one exercise his best known art."

This Sporting Life is dedicated to most of us, the amateurs of sport, who know at firsthand the pleasures of play and the frustration of limiting factors—fatigue, weather, injury, one's self.

There are poems here about those who beat the odds, nature's as well as the game's, the sports heroes who deliver when placed at high risk; at bat with two out, bases loaded; leaping for the spiral on fourth down, tie game and the clock running out; sticking the back flip on the balance beam with the tournament in the balance.

The element of risk is not only part of the thrill for players and fans but a reminder of the fact that running, swimming, riding, hunting, fishing, the martial arts—in fact, most sports—were not originally pastimes but essential exercises of survival skills.

These poems record the emotional dynamics of team play, the relationships of coaches and players, the bonding among team-mates, and the rivalries that flare when people are divided into opposing teams. During the game, winning is not an abstract emotion but a passionate be-all and end-all. Few other situations, except perhaps war, focus our intense desire to compete and to conquer so sharply. The fact that such strong negative emotions can be successfully diverted to the playing field and the stadium for a restricted period of time is a compelling rationale for the staging of regular international games.

Human beings are born into the language of movement; we speak body language before any other, learning its signals and subtleties from infancy. The contemporary American poems in this anthology give vivid language to wordless experience, represent our delight in physicality, the joining of body and will in coordinated response. Poetry is, after all, another ancient game.

—Emilie Buchwald / Ruth Roston

This
Sporting
Life

Life Is Water

"I tell a friend that life is water."

—Janice M. Lynch, Excerpts from "Sixty-Four Caprices for a Long Distance Swimmer: Notes on Swimming 100 Miles"

Maxine Kumin

400-METER FREE STYLE

THE GUN full swing the swimmer catapults and
   cracks
                                  s
                                   i
                                  x

feet away onto that perfect glass he catches at
a
n
 d

throws behind him scoop after scoop cunningly
   moving
                              t
                                h
                                 e

water back to move him forward. Thrift is his
wonderful
  s
e
  c

ret; he has schooled out all extravagance. No muscle
                                   r
                                    i
                                  p
ples without compensation wrist cock to heel snap to
h
i
  s

mobile mouth that siphons in the air that nurtures
                                h
                                 i
                                 m

at half an inch above sea level so to speak.
  T
h
  e

astonishing whites of the soles of his feet rise
                                                a
                                                 n
                                                  d

salute us on the turns. He flips, converts, and is gone
   a
 l
   l
in one. We watch him for signs. His arms are steady
      at
                                                       t
                                                        h
                                                         e

catch, his cadent feet tick in the stretch, they know
   t
 h
   e
lesson well. Lungs know, too; he does not list for
                                                  a
                                                   i
                                                    r
he drives along on little sips carefully expended
   b
 u
   t
that plum red heart pumps hard cries hurt now soon
                                                   i
                                                    t
                                                     s
near one more and makes its final surge
                TIME:4:25:9

ALIXA DOOM

SNORKELING IN THE CARIBBEAN

Flapping flippered feet
I enter my mask
and my breath
filling my head like a surf
I wobble weightless
as a windflower.
How my body has longed
to forget itself this way!
Tiny intense blue fish
like a flotilla of fingers
divide for my passage
and join again
with the indifference
of a river.

Parrot fish, french angels, groupers
aloof as foreign children.
In the round eye of the angel
there is no woman, wife, winter.
Years of coats, boots
fall without a syllable.
Elastic as a cloud
I loll above fish,
their hot blossom colors
pulsing
in a stall of coral.

I have always known
the end was this way,
something I would sink in
rather than ascend to.
The floor of a sea,
single wings of fish,
and my breath
which is all
I need to know
of myself.

SWIMMER

I

Observe how he negotiates his way
With trust and the least violence, making
The stranger friend, the enemy ally.
The depth that could destroy gently supports him.
With water he defends himself from water.
Danger he leans on, rests in. The drowning sea
Is all he has between himself and drowning.

II

What lover ever lay more mutually
With his beloved, his always-reaching arms
Stroking in smooth and powerful caresses?
Some drown in love as in dark water, and some
By love are strongly held as the green sea
Now holds the swimmer. Indolently he turns
To float. — The swimmer floats, the lover sleeps.

MAXINE KUMIN

TO SWIM, TO BELIEVE
Centre College, Danville, Kentucky

The beautiful excess of Jesus on the waters
is with me now in the Boles Natatorium.
This bud of me exults, giving witness:

these flippers that rose up to be arms.
These strings drawn to be fingers.
Legs plumped to make my useful fork.

Each time I tear this seam to enter,
all that I carry is taken from me,
shucked in the dive.

Lovers, children, even words go under.
Matters of dogma spin off in the freestyle
earning that mid-pool spurt, like faith.

Where have I come from? Where am I going?
What do I translate, gliding back and forth
erasing my own stitch marks in this lane?

Christ on the lake was not thinking
where the next heel-toe went.
God did him a dangerous favor
whereas Peter, the thinker, sank.

The secret is in the relenting,
the partnership. I let my body work

accepting the dangerous favor
from this king-size pool of waters.
Together I am supplicant. I am bride.

WILLIAM MEISSNER

THE REUNION: SWIMMING

To save yourself,
think of your swimming body as the straightest line you can
     imagine.
Amid this sway of circles
make each motion perfect:
blend your fingers into a fin,
stretch your legs into long pink roads.

At first you'll find yourself climbing waves
like endless stairways, gulping water
bitter as history.
But think of your body
as something in flight—an arrow, perhaps.
Soon you'll forget that you're swimming
at all; you'll inhale normally
as when you lie sleeping on your side,
the puppet strings of dreams
tugging at your wrists.

You tell yourself you'll know the shore instantly
by the smooth touch of sand, the weeds
wrapping around your fingers
like lost pet snakes, green rings.

But somehow the land keeps its distance from you,
drawing away, a wave moving backwards.
This small lake widens
and widens like a mouth
that has forgotten
how to close.

You begin to believe water
is nothing more than
a thick, heavy air
we humans
must learn how to breathe

You look again toward shore.
See the one small tree on the sandy beach,
the bony arm waving,
the flag of a continent
you will always see just ahead of you
but never visit.

PATRICIA GOEDICKE

IN THE OCEAN

At first my mother would be shy
Leaving my lame father behind

But then she would tuck up her bathing cap
And fly into the water like a dolphin,

Slippery as bamboo she would bend
Everywhere, everywhere I remember

For though he would often be criticizing her,
Blaming her, finding fault

Behind her back he would talk about her
All through our childhood, to me
            and my sister,

She rarely spoke against him

Except to take us by the hand
In the ocean we would laugh together

As we never did, on dry land

Because he was an invalid
Usually she was silent

But this once, on her deathbed

Hearing me tell it she remembered
Almost before I did, and she smiled

One more time to think of it,
How, with the waves crashing at our feet

Slithering all over her wet skin

We would rub against her like minnows
We would flow between her legs, in the surf

Smooth as spaghetti she would hold us
Close against her like small polliwogs climbing

All over her as if she were a hill,
A hill that moved, our element

But hers also, safe
In the oval of each other's arms

This once she would be weightless
As guiltless, utterly free

Of all but what she loved
Smoothly, with no hard edges,

My long beautiful mother
In her white bathing cap, crowned

Like an enormous lily

Over the brown arrow of her body,
The limber poles of her legs,

The strong cheekbones, and the shadows
Like fluid lavender, everywhere

In a rainbow of breaking foam

Looping and sliding through the waves
We would swim together as one

Mother and sea calves gliding,
Floating as if all three of us were flying.

JANICE M. LYNCH

EXCERPTS FROM

SIXTY-FOUR CAPRICES FOR A LONG-DISTANCE SWIMMER: NOTES ON SWIMMING 100 MILES

1. A friend asks why I swim. Why not a movie? A drink? Dinner? I answer that I swim for strength, for a rippling tricep and a dimple in my thigh. I hide the lie with a stroke: I swim for the silence of water.

2. An older woman stopped swimming and watched me. What a graceful stroke! What she loved, of course, was the mirrored beauty of her youth — the forgotten pleasure of her toughened skin.

3. The water undulates like a womb I do not remember. My fingers poke through for life. The air is unfamiliar.

4. I tell a friend that life is water. With a pretended fluidity his heart mimics the ocean — but he cannot swim. He answers that a cell full of water explodes.

5. Seventy-year old women stand naked in the locker room. Some use walkers, others have artificial hips, scarred legs and missing breasts, still, they love this morning swim with the distant sun rising.

6. In these women, I witness how I too will age. I avert my eyes, move to far lanes and other shadows.

7. I swim past men to prove my strength — after years of "throwing like a girl" — I lap them twice.

10. I tap slower swimmers' feet to pass them. Their skin startles me, as though I've come upon schools of spot running south for winter.

15. I dream of fire. I dream of fire and combustion. The things water does not heal.

17. How do we breathe underwater? A moment without air is magic. Through goggles, I watch the bubbles insist on my life.

18. Fifty others swim in the pool. Water molecules vibrate with our personalities. I swallow each person's breath, yet remain alone.

21. This—is—the—point—where I always—want to stop. Turn—legs—ache—lungs heave—arms weary—the distance—is forever—force the push—break water.

22. Every morning, two crows perch near the pool's glass doors and peck madly at their reflections. When no one watches, I jump out of the pool and run, arms raised and mouth squawking, to chase them away.

23. Then all three of us jump—the crows with fright to the sky—and me, chilled, to the diving well.

24. Every other breath my face sculpts a water mask.

26. Blood throbs, echoing the physics of water and sound. It sets up a rhythm between myself and other swimmers.

29. At a certain angle, the hand slices sheets of water. This requires a force the body is unaware of, even as pounds of water move away like the curtain rising over the first act.

30. What does it mean to drown in a dream? Is there the hope of bellying-up like a fish? Are we forced to forget breathing?

31. Some days there is no difference between sleep and dreams, between swimming and drowning, water and air.

36. After a winter of depression, inches of sadness float across the pool.

37. Sometimes, breathing, the heaviness of my own life amazes me. Sucking on air, I consume the world.

40. Breaststroke beads the surface like mercury on skin. I'm a skeet barely touching water, needing it only to serve my own motion.

41. I try to describe my father, but he eludes me, fast as a rock skipping the ocean. I try to describe my mother, but she is too much myself—familiar as oxygen gurgling about my waist.

42. I learned to walk because my sister was born and I knew that I would never be carried again.

43. I learned to swim because my father threw me in the deep end and shouted "Swim!"

44. I sweat in the water and my face is cooled, ice cooled on ice.

45. As children, my sisters and I linked arms with my father and ran into the Atlantic, afraid only of letting go and coming up in some other ocean.

46. A man paralyzed from the waist down swims slowly, his legs quivering with the dream of motion. In a dream that my strength reaches him through the water, I swim faster, give up another length.

47. At dawn the moon fits the socket of the sky like a great white bulb.

61. When I swim I am the totality of water. I am hydrogen and oxygen. I am pure strength and energy.

64. I shed the water's silk cocoon for the certain embrace of air; my body emerges from the pool, form from cut crystal.

HANDICAPPED CHILDREN SWIMMING

For Lamar

A measure of freedom. Mike, floating,
would not manage so without
the red life-jacket but would sink,

messy as weed; but with it
lies, weak, like a shirt,
and the eyes, and the tongue

uncontrolled, extended, show
the delight it is to be
horizontal on water, strapped there

by nothing but sunlight. Connie,
who otherwise moves with crutches
and stiff braces, is strong

through water. Becky, seeing always
badly, lies washed by the sense
of her own fragility, liking

the help of warm hands. Gregg
rides and plucks at the water
while Danny makes his own music

in his mind as he lilts
completely quiet. Mike's delight
opens like a flower as he floats.

He doesn't know he is floating
now in this poem. I have
nothing in fact to sustain him

and I know he will never stand
up alone. But whatever sustains
the children here is so important;

inflamed with the success
of water, released, they mingle
and soften there, as wax

on wetness, limp as wet bread
on water's kindness. Those fingers
can grasp as competently at air

and water as mine. Their bodies
are milky and do not need
cleansing, except from deformity.

Water cannot wash their
awkwardness from them, water is
simple, and their defects difficult;

but they ride for a while, never
as free as the times they fly
in dreams, over the cliffs

harvesting in the sea, the bats
exquisite with radar, but
something, a measure of freedom.

And Mike is lucid on water,
still physically cryptic, physically
glinting, but Mike has grace

for a while, this is his best
floating since before birth,
where he lay bunched like any

other unformed—encircled, contained
his mother not knowing the
uncontrol of those limbs that

threshed and kicked at her
from out of that orchard of water,
Light strolls among them, padding

healthy, firm, as these imperfect
children perch rolling in the foliage
of water, shifting to new flowerings

of face, though their limbs are
weeds. The shock comes when you see
the muscular men who played

with them in the pool carry them
in huddles from the pool, sunlight
spreading its crime on them.

DELIVERANCE

Putting in below the dam, watching
the water boil and seethe over rocks,
ledges, feeling fear churn like a stopper
in my stomach. In an open canoe,
we must plot like chess players:
strategies, moves, pries, and draws.

To float with the mainstream is madness,
moving directly in the current,
paddling like a windmill:
rockfilled pillows wait, and
you stick, spin, and swamp
down the way to watery sleep.
Or fallen trees block the way,
the current lures you under like a siren,
and the mad black branches bring you down.

No, canoeing's a delicate dance:
to move forward, you must go back,
holding the angle, bracing high or low.
You measure strength not in miles,
but how the river's played,
like a fish on a singing line.
And even though the souse holes yawn,
your eye, quick as a kingfisher,
spots the eddies where you rest.
And all around, the rapids roar like chaos,
and far ahead, standing waves
dance like a symphony,
and you, with your paddle,
have created a garden from the grave.

SAILING

After years by the ocean
a man finds he learns to sail
in the middle of the country,
on the surface of a small lake with a woman's name
in a small boat with one sail.

All summer he skims back and forth
across the open, blue eye of the midwest.
The wind comes in from the northeast
most days and the man learns
how to seem to go against it, learns
of the natural always crouched
in the shadow of the unnatural.

Sometimes the wind stops
and the man is becalmed —
just like the old traders who sat for days
in the Doldrums on the thin skin of the ocean,
nursing their scurveys
and grumbling over short grog rations.

And the man learns a certain language:
he watches the luff, beats windward, comes
hard-about, finally gets
port and starboard straight.

All summer, between the soft, silt bottom
and the blue sheath of the sky, he glides
back and forth across the modest lake
with the woman's name.

And at night
he dreams of infinite flat surfaces,
of flying at incredible speed,
one hand on the tiller, one on the mainsheet, leaning
far out over the sparkling surface, the sail
a transparent membrane, the wind
with its silent howl, a force
moving him from his own heart.

ON WEATHERING GALES

Whether to rig the sea anchor
from stem or from stern
depends on the cut of the hull.

If the line is streamed from the bow
the boat may lie broadside to the waves
or make sternway too fast, jam the rudder.

If you rig from the stern, the following seas
can flood into the cockpit—you'll swamp.
In either case, tow ropes chafe, fray and break.

Run for port—assuming you know
where you are on the chart—you risk
going aground, or smashing up at the lighthouse.

Mainsail and mizzen are reefed.
Still you heel more with each swell.
Shortening sail is no longer enough.

Then strip the masts,
lash the helm, lie a'hull
in the troughs between crests.

Bare poles still respond to the wind.
Slowly you reach on through the seas.
Perhaps you can ride out the night.

The question is, why
are you out here at all?
Yet you know:

As soon as you're dry and repaired
you will set sail again,
still stalking the perfect wind.

INTO THE WIND

Away,
    out
   beyond
  the soiling
  hands of land,
 you go to lay your
head in the lap of the
waves, to float in womb-rest
and stillness. But Poseidon has
breathed life into your sails, and
up you leap to the rigging to assert
your own course, white sheets luffing
like a trembling heart. Hard to lee,
you duck and gather power, drawing in
line, leaning out just far enough to
tease the waters, as your loving
hands cajole the fickle wind
    to
    do
as you may desire, tacking
with its strength, never
spitting into its eye
 •

Climbing the Air

"We were different when we returned to earth."

      —Charles Ghigna, "DIVERS"

AUSTIN STRAUS

THE JUGGLER

The only juggler in history able
to . . . juggle. . . 10 balls or 8 plates was the Italian
Enrico Rastelli. . . born in Samara, Russia, on
December 19, 1896, and died in Bergamo, Italy, on
December 13, 1931.
    —Guinness Book of World Records

Died
at thirty-five, not even.

Did juggling
do him in?

Maybe that eleventh ball
or ninth plate

he just couldn't orbit
with the others

or the tension of sustaining
ten or eight

night after night
show after show

broke his heart
like a dish.

LINES

Anchoring, I watched him climb,
His legs still smooth, his ringless hands
Grasping, inching at the cliff,
His eyes turned upward toward my own,
My own smiling downward at my son.
Trying not to look beyond
At what lay a thousand feet below
We climbed, he climbed, his hair blown wild,
His fear clenched tight between his teeth,
Our courage on raw fingertips.

And then a piton went. He fell
Into the space that welcomed him
And toward the rocks that waited. . . .
My hand, not knowing, reached far out,
Reached empty into empty air.
The mountain turned him upside down.
And then the falling stopped.

He dangled there —

A diver diving half a sky
His body limp,
Suspended on a nylon line
Drawn taut, mere twisting from his waist
To mine, from which that life,
Now saved, now caught,
Now breathing far beyond my own,
Had come.

PARALLEL BARS

*Like the rings, the parallel bars require great upper body
strength. Moves should be performed both above and below
the bars with no more than three hesitations or stops.*

the sun reveals the galaxy of dust
that drifts in the gym

some days there is an empty nest
in everyone's mood
their eyes stare out from
the darkside of the ground
you must work your way out
grip the bars and pull yourself into the balance
    of a handstand
swing into the currents of dust

each routine is a journey
to a special place
the rails become condor wings
that open the ocean
where the body blooms into a thousand leaves

there are still moments
when you can see the desert
three cows buried in the sand
their bones
the faint outline of constellations
sometimes at dusk
we are just silhouettes
our bodies outlined with light
as if the sun was at our feet
a child
we bend down to
and so
we rotate in a current of gravity
it is hard to die
because we are birds
who know the joy of falling

FROM THE XXIII SUMMER OLYMPICS, THE POET AS REPORTER

XVI. A Kind of Thanks

Another high jumper
after an attempt that succeeds,
looking up from the cushions
looking up at the bar, still up there, if swaying,
and applauded
> the bar
> the sun
> the open air
> sweat
> and the earth
from which momentarily he successfully had fled.

DAVID ALLAN EVANS

POLE VAULTER

The approach to the bar
is everything

unless I have counted
my steps   hit my markers
feel up to it   I refuse
to follow through
I am committed to beginnings
or to nothing

planting the pole
at runway's end
jolts me
out of sprinting
I take off   kicking in
and up   my whole weight
trying the frailty
of fiberglass

never forcing myself
trusting it is right
to be taken to the end
of tension   poised for
the powerful thrust to
fly me beyond expectation

near the peak
I roll my thighs inward
arch my back   clearing
as much of the bar as I can
(knowing the best jump
can be cancelled
by a careless elbow)

and open my hands

HIGH JUMPER

Looking at the standards,
he closes his eyes,
imagining himself
a pure figure following
a precise mathematical arc
away from the bar,

    and everything slows,

then he begins to close,
whip back,
gathering speed
as he shoves the weight
of the universe down through
his foot, his right arm
shot upward in a victory signal
toward heaven,
his right shoulder suddenly liquid
bending in on itself,
his hip bones thrust out —

    then everything stops.

and his body, floating,
knows nothing more
than itself,
is calm, severe, solid, yet light

    (what *is* the sum of the length
    of ourselves?)

and stays that way,
with no time over it,
hurrying.

DEAR MOM

Please don't tell my mother
I'm a rodeo cowboy. She thinks I play
piano at the whorehouse in Wallace, Idaho.

The night that devil danced on me
I know how you barely peeked
between fingers and beads. You heard
the hard play-by-play
announcer cawing from the crow's nest,
above the cowboy holler and dusk,
how I was hung and being drug
by a bronc no one could stop. No,
dad should not have brought his gun,
and I doubt your rosary
will salvage me from hell. You bet
I can remember
how you massaged my gums
with homemade hooch
to ease the teething,
how you never dreamed
that twenty-three years later
a palomino bronc named Moonshine
would leave me toothless in Missoula.

DIVERS

We were different when we returned to earth.
Too alone in our fall to forget,
We lost all trust in the touch of gentle hands.
The dropped baby in us grew.

We listened too long to a thinner wind,
Climbed too close to a hollow sun,
Stood one by one in the cockpit's open door,
Left our mothered souls in the fading steel
Of a Cessna's shaking belly,
Stepped into a hand-less world,
Stretched the corners of our eyes until they spit,
Watched an anvil earth fly up at us,
Took our own umbilical cord in hand and ripped,
And fell like frightened spiders
Who spin out frantic silk that clings to only air.

Our jarred bodies lay on a sudden fist of clay,
Unwound themselves from web and line
And carried the dead fish in our feet
Away to dreams of distant seas.

Racquets

"Your arm flung up, like an easy sail . . . "

—Maxine Kumin, "Prothalamion"

SAM ALBERT

AFTER A GAME OF SQUASH

And I thought of how impossibly alone we were,
up in the room where the lockers are and the showers,
he with wiping the sweat from his face and head,
and I bending over, loosening the laces from my sneakers.

We had just finished this long game of squash.
Then, we were much closer, smashing the same ball,
lurching forward, out-maneuvering each other
hard down the sidelines, death to the opponent.

It was a battle, the killer's eye in the middle
of the round black ball, two men struggling
to find each other out, what made each one's mind work,
and with what heart each fell to the long odds.

And when the game was over we thanked each other generously,
complimented one the other on his skill, his finesse.
And I thought of how impossibly alone we were,
up in the room where the lockers are and the showers.

CONTEST

*"If I played myself last year,
I'd beat her."*
—Martina Navratilova

I let roots pull foot tendons
down,
until I am just about
here.
I know what
I can get away with.
When I am tired,
I stop.

The young ones
run circles around me,
seem translucent,
ineffective.
They do everything
wrong,
make mistakes,
lack experience.

That is how I keep up
with them.

THE MIDNIGHT TENNIS MATCH

Note: *In midnight tennis each player gets three serves
rather than the usual two.*

You are tired
of this maudlin country club
and you are tired of his insults.
You'd like to pummel his forehead
with a Schweppes bottle
in the sauna, but instead
you agree, this time,
to meet him at midnight
on the tennis court.

When you get there
you can't see him
but you know he is waiting
on the other side of the net.
You consider briefly
his reputation.

You have first serve
so you run toward the net
and dive over it.
You land hard on your face.
It's not a good serve: looking up
you can barely see his white shorts
gleam in the darkness.

You get up, go back
to your side of the net
and dive over again.
This time you slide
to within a few feet of him.
Now you can make out his ankles,
the glint of the moon
on his white socks.

Your last serve is the best:
your chin stops one inch
from the tip of his sneakers.
Pinheads of blood
bloom across your chest.
You feel good crawling
back to your side again.

Now it is his turn
and as he runs toward the net
you know he's the fastest man
you've ever seen.

His dive is of course flawless.
He soars by you,
goes completely off the court
and onto the lawn,
demolishing a few lounge chairs.
To finish, he slides
brilliantly onto the veranda.

You go up and sit beside him
and somehow
you don't feel too humiliated:
he is still unconscious.
At least now you know why
he is undefeated. It's
his sensitive, yet brutal, contempt.
With a similar contempt
you pour a gallon of water on his face.
He still has two more serves—

BAD SPORT

Prairie women quilted.
She saves other scraps
for soup stock, garden
mulch, maybe a poem.
Always a way to weave
minutes into hours.
Some women know how
to leap over the net
at birth. Good game.

She dreams of acting badly.
Slamming the racquet down.
Hanging up hard. Envy
of women who rag men out
for ugly glances. Why not
shout that's cheating,
stop, call time.
Some women know
when to throw things out.

ON THE TENNIS COURT AT NIGHT

We step out on the green rectangle
in moonlight; the lines glow,
which for many have been the only lines
of justice. We remember
the thousand trajectories the air has erased
of that close-contested last set—
blur of volleys, soft arcs of drop shots,
huge ingrown loops of lobs with topspin
which went running away, crosscourts recrossing
down to each sweet (and in exact proportion, bitter)
❂ in Talbert and Olds' *The Game of Doubles in Tennis.*
The breeze has carried them off but we still hear
the mutters, the doublefaulter's groans,
cries of "Deuce!" or "Love two!",
squeak of tennis shoes, grunt of overreaching,
all dozen extant tennis quips—"Just out!"
or, "About right for you?" or, "Want to change partners?"
and *baaah* of sheep translated very occasionally
into *thonk* of well-hit ball, among the pure
right angles and unhesitating lines
of this arena where every man grows old
pursuing that repertoire of perfect shots,
darkness already in his strokes,
even in death cramps waving an arm back and forth
to the disgust of the night nurse
(to whom the wife whispers, "Well,
at least I always knew where he was!");
and smiling; and a few hours later found dead—
the smile still in place but the ice bag
left on the brow now inexplicably
Scotchtaped to the right elbow—causing
all those bright trophies to slip permanently,
though not in fact much farther, out of reach,
all except the thick-bottomed young man
about to doublefault in soft metal on the windowsill:
"Runner-Up Men's Class B Consolation Doubles
St. Johnsbury Kiwanis Tennis Tournament 1969". . .
Clouds come over the moon;
all the lines go out. November last year

in Lyndonville: it is getting dark,
snow starts falling, Zander Rubin wobble-twists
his worst serve out of the black woods behind him,
Stan Albro lobs into a gust of snow,
Don Bredes smashes at where the ball theoretically
could be coming down, the snow blows down
and swirls about our legs, darkness flows
across a disappearing patch of green-painted asphalt
in the north country, where four men,
half-volleying, poaching, missing, grunting,
begging mercy of their bones, hold their ground,
as winter comes on, all the winters to come.

PROTHALAMION

The far court opens for us all July.
Your arm, flung up like an easy sail bellying,
comes down on the serve in a blue piece of sky
barely within reach, and you, following,
tip forward on the smash. The sun sits still
on the hard white canvas lip of the net. Five-love.
Salt runs behind my ears at thirty-all.
At game, I see the sweat that you're made of.
We improve each other, quickening so by noon
that the white game moves itself, the universe
contracted to the edge of the dividing line
you toe against—limbering for your service,
arm up, swiping the sun time after time—
and the square I live in, measured out with lime.

Play Ball

"The ball would lift
light as a wish, . . . "

—Carl Lindner, "WHEN I GOT IT RIGHT"

MISSOULA SOFTBALL TOURNAMENT

This summer, most friends out of town
and no wind playing flash and dazzle
in the cottonwoods, music of the Clark Fork stale,
I've gone back to the old ways of defeat,
the softball field, familiar dust and thud,
pitcher winging drops and rises, and wives,
the beautiful wives in the stands, basic, used,
screeching runners home, infants unattended
in the dirt. A long triple sails into right center.
Two men on. Shouts from dugout: go, Ron, go.
Life is better run from. Distance to the fence,
both foul lines and dead center, is displayed.

I try to steal the tricky manager's signs.
Is hit-and-run the pulling of the ear?
The ump gives pitchers too much low inside.
Injustice? Fraud? Ancient problems focus
in the heat. Bad hop on routine grounder.
Close play missed by the team you want to win.
Players from the first game, high on beer,
ride players in the field. Their laughter
falls short of the wall. Under lights, the moths
are momentary stars, and wives, the beautiful wives
in the stands now take the interest they once feigned,
oh, long ago, their marriage just begun, years
of helping husbands feel important just begun,
the scrimping, the anger brought home evenings
from degrading jobs. This poem goes out to them.

Is steal-of-home the touching of the heart?
Last pitch. A soft fly. A can of corn
the players say. Routine, like mornings,
like the week. They shake hands on the mound.
Nice grab on that shot to left. Good game. Good game.
Dust rotates in their headlight beams.
The wives, the beautiful wives are with their men.

THE BASE STEALER

Poised between going on and back, pulled
Both ways taut like a tightrope-walker,
Fingertips pointing the opposites,
Now bouncing tiptoe like a dropped ball
Or a kid skipping rope, come on, come on,
Running a scattering of steps sidewise,
How he teeters, skitters, tingles, teases,
Taunts them, hovers like an ecstatic bird,
He's only flirting, crowd him, crowd him,
Delicate, delicate, delicate, delicate — now!

MYSTERY BASEBALL

No one knows the man who throws out the season's first ball.
　His face has never appeared in the newspapers,
　　except in crowd scenes, blurred.
　Asked his name, he mumbles something
　　about loneliness,
　　about the beginnings of hard times.

Each team fields an extra, tenth man.
　This is the invisible player,
　　assigned to no particular position.
　Runners edging off base feel a tap on their shoulders,
　　turn, see no one.
　Or a batter, the count against him, will hear whispered
　　in his ear vague, dark
　　rumors of his wife, and go down.

Vendors move through the stands
　selling unmarked sacks,
　never disclosing their contents,
　never having been told.
　People buy, hoping.

Pitchers stay busy
　getting signs.
　They are everywhere.

One man rounds third base, pumping hard,
　and is never seen again.
　Teammates and relatives wait years at the plate,
　　uneasy, fearful.

An outfielder goes for a ball on the warning track.
  He leaps into the air and keeps rising,
    beyond himself, past
    the limp flag.
  Days later he is discovered,
    descended, wandering dazed
    in centerfield.

Deep under second base lives an old man,
  bearded, said to be
  a hundred. All through the game,
  players pull at the bills of their caps,
  acknowledging him.

GARY GILDNER

IN MY MEANEST DAYDREAM

I am throwing hard again
clipping corners, shaving
letters, dusting off
the heavy sticker crowding clean-up
clean down to his smelly socks—
& when my right spike hits
the ground he's had his look
already & gets
hollow in the belly—
in my meanest daydream I let fly
a sweet stream of spit, my catcher
pops his mitt
& grins
& calls me baby.

HALVARD JOHNSON

AMERICANS PLAYING SLOW-PITCH SOFTBALL AT AN AIRBASE NEAR KUNSAN, SOUTH KOREA

—Early September
The first game of
the evening begins
about five-thirty.

The men (not that
only men play—
one team has

a female catcher)
finish their work
on whatever they

work on—
correspondence,
water mains, Phantoms—

get out of one uniform,
into another, and come
out to the ballpark.

The lights go on early.
By eight here it's totally
dark. Half an hour earlier

the sky was a tangle
of rose, magenta,
lavender, as the sun

went down in China,
beyond the Yellow Sea.
Brisk wind tonight—

raises the infield dirt,
whips it into narrowed eyes
of batter, catcher, umpire,

the three or four spectators
in the bleachers behind them.
A regulation seven-inning

game is played, unless one
team is so far out in front
that the ten-run rule

is invoked, ending
the game after five. A ball
the size of a small

grapefruit is lofted
into the air, a slight
backspin making it

seem to drift and float
down toward the plate.
No easy hit. The batter

has to apply his own
muscle to put it anywhere.
This batsman clips the top

and bounces to the third
baseman, who fires to first
for an easy out. He shrugs

and jogs to the dugout.
The next batter flies out,
and the game ends 15-zip

after five full innings.
Another two teams take the field.
Some of the players stand

by to watch the second game,
but most wander off,
concerned with other things.

The bleachers are fuller now —
a rowdier crowd, raring for action.
Crisp evening air. Korean girlfriends

cuddle close for warmth. An airman
pops open a beer. Behind their
backs a pair of Phantoms

roar into the sky, their afterburners
glowing as they lift from the runway,
vanish into black clouds. Uncertain

weather tonight, a stiff wind, high
scudding clouds. A tricky weather
system reaching north to

the DMZ, east to the Sea of Japan,
south to the East China Sea.
Typhoon Orchid approaches Okinawa,

far to the southeast. Possibly
this is all a part of that. Inning
after inning goes by, vanishing

into a past that exists only on paper.
Hits, runs, and errors go down
in the league's record book,

but screw the past, we're having
fun tonight. Neither the pitcher,
the fliers, nor the Korean

women in the stands
remember or care about a war
that happened thirty years ago.

It's the girls' fathers who have
the bad dreams, wake in terror in
the night. Their grandfathers, too.

They'll all support General Chun
and pray he'll protect them
from devils. A friend of mine

in Europe once wrote a poem
about memory and the historical
imagination, which ended

with these lines:
"Our assignment is to remember,
to deliver blows."

No American could have written that.
We live our lives inning by inning,
season by season, war by war.

I'll end this in an American way —
with the words of the great black,
American pitcher, Satchel Paige:

    "Don't look back.
    Something may be
    gaining on you."

Emilio De Grazia

PASTTIME

A girl, nine years of wonder
Still on her face,
Stands directly on the bag at third
Running amazed fingers along the wrinkles
Of my old leather mitt.
It is the bottom of the ninth,
And everywhere in the world
The bases are loaded.

SUSAN FIRER

A NIGHT GAME IN MENOMONIE PARK

A night game in Menomonie Park,
Where the ladies hit the large white balls
like stars through the night they roll
like angelfood cake batter folded through devilsfood.
Again, I want to hear the fans' empty beer cans
being crushed — new ones hissing open.
"You're a gun, Anna"
"She can't hit"
"Lay it on."
Oh, run, swift softball women
under the lights the Kiwanis put in.
Be the wonderful sliding night
animals I remember. Remind me constantly
of human error and redemption.
Hit
ball after ball to the lip of the field
while the lake flies fall like confetti
under the park's night lights.
Sunlight Dairy Team, remember me
as you lift your bats,
pump energy into
them bats, whirling circular as helicopter
blades above your heads.
Was it the ball Julie on the Honey "B" Tavern Team
hit toward my head that made me so soft-
ball crazy that right in the middle of a tune
by Gentleman Jim's Orchestra, here in Bingo/Polka
Heaven at Saint Mary of Czestochowa's annual Kielbasa
Festival, I go homesick for Oshkosh women's softball?
I order another Kielbasa and wonder
if Donna will stay on third next game or
again run head down wild into Menomonie homeplate.
Play louder, Gentleman Jim.
Saint Mary of Czestochowa throws a swell festival, but
Oshkosh women's softball — that's a whole other ballgame.

COUPLET

Old Timer's Day, Fenway Park, 1 May 1982

When the tall puffy
figure wearing number
nine starts
late for the fly ball,
laboring forward
like a lame truckhorse
startled by a gartersnake,
—this old fellow
whose body we remember
as sleek and nervous
as a filly's—

and barely catches it
in his glove's
tip, we rise
and applaud weeping:
On a green field
we observe the ruin
of even the bravest
body, as Odysseus
wept to glimpse
among shades the shadow
of Achilles.

FLY BALL

A fly ball
has nothing of flight about it
it's pushed out there
its trajectory absolute
as the slap of the bat

but no one has ever seen
a ball go into the glove
it's true
follow the arc
unblinking the slow climb up the last leg
of the mountain   the raising of a flag   salute
the sure sail home to the cup
of the mitt

suddenly the field breaks up
everyone running the same way
a terrible accident
Christ has landed
at International Airport
your presence is required

no it's just the game   over
you missed it
in that last inch
the ball disappears

in fact there's a moment when the ball never enters the
        glove
it decides to cock a wing
veer to the south
    so long folks   I'm off on a jet-
    stream the sweet south
    wind in my wingpits   we're all going
    all U.S. fly balls going to take off
    like popcorn roll down the coast
    and bloom like migratory monarchs
    on the trees of Argentina

no it's still coming
a single headlight   you below it
on the tracks

the ball ballooning
rides clear as an onion
breaking from its skin
that terrible moon

coming
damn thing never stops
blazing with possibilities
and it's yours   you claim it
whether you want it or not
it will come   what matters
is where you are

BASKET CATCH

It was in '58, the year they moved out,
the year Mays had his windows smashed, midseason,
for hitting only .329, the year Toothpick
Jones lost his no-hitter in the bottom of the ninth,
that I became a fan.

I was seven.
My Dad was forty and liked to carry on
about Johnny Antonelli.
Night games, he'd pace the breakfast room floor
with his fiddle, and when the going got bad,
when the Redlegs had runners on the corners,
he'd blister a few double stops,
a towering *partita*,
as if he was Kluszewski himself in the on deck circle.
Look at that lumber.
Stop him Johnny.

Occasionally, in the middle innings,
there'd be this strange calm come over him.
Was he contemplating his life — that dance
between emotion and restraint —
now that Davenport was caught napping at first,
and Felipe Alou left standing, bowlegged at the plate?
There is no solitude like baseball.

My father's miseries arrived with the early summer
as the Giants went into their June swoon,
and Arthur Fiedler came to town.
Stuck in the pit, three weeks
of show tunes, waltzes, fairy music.
Enough to ruin a man's soul.
He hated the crowds.
They're the lowest common denominator,
the easy listeners, the lousy pretzel nibblers.

He loved the bleachers though.
HEY, BURGIE!
Especially when the lowly Phillies came to town.
BURGERMEISTER!
Let 'em pitch Robin Roberts.

A LOAF OF BREAD!
Let Ashburn hit for the cycle.
A POUND OF MEAT!
We'll still take 'em.
AND ALL THE MUSTARD YOU CAN EAT!
HOT DOGGIES!!!

We were out in right field, one day,
when Willie Kirkland misjudged a fly.
The crowd all over him. A fat man
full of beer, chanting:
dumb nigger, dumb nigger, dumb nigger
Reluctantly, Kirkland began to climb the fence
'til Mays loped over from center and cooed at him.
This is how the world is, rookie.
HEY, BURGIE!

I was a child, sucking my thumb
against all that was harsh,
peeking through the planks of bleachers
to that horrid place little boys
could fall to in a flutter
of hotdog wrapper and old scorecards.
My Dad glared at fat man,
and led me by the hand to centerfield,
called to Mays in a voice
only he and I could hear.
Give us a basket catch, Willie.

HALVARD JOHNSON

THE EXTRA-INNING BALLGAME

Wanting things to go on forever,
yet craving the apocalypse.
Reading the last few pages at one word a minute.
Wanting to teeter forever at the brink of the abyss,
and loving every minute of it.

The solid single lashed over second.
A shortstop's arm, just long enough to catch it.

Richard Hugo

LETTER TO MANTSCH FROM HAVRE

Dear Mike: We didn't have a chance. Our starter had no change
and second base had not been plugged since early in July.
How this town turned out opening night of the tournament
to watch their Valley Furniture team wipe us, the No-
Name Tavern of Missoula, out. Remember Monty Holden,
ace Havre pitcher, barber, hero of the Highline, and his
tricky "catch-this" windup? First inning, when you hit that shot,
one on, the stands went stone. It still rockets the night.
I imagine it climbing today, somewhere in the universe,
lovelier than a girl climbs on a horse and lovelier than star.
We lost that game. No matter. Won another. Lost again
and went back talking fondly of your four home runs,
triple and single in three games, glowing in the record book.
I came back after poems. They ask me today, here in Havre,
who's that player you brought here years ago, the hitter?
So few of us are good at what we do, and what we do,
well done or not, seems futile. I'm trying to find Monty
Holden's barber shop. I want to tell him style in anything,
pitching, hitting, cutting hair, is worth our trying even
if we fail. And when that style, the graceful compact swing
leaves the home crowd hearing its blood and the ball roars off
in night like determined moon, it is our pleasure
to care about something well done. If he doesn't understand
more than the final score, if he says, "After all, we won,"
I'll know my hair will not look right after he's done,
what little hair I have, what little time. And I'll drive home
knowing his windup was all show, glad I was there years back,
that I was lucky enough to be there when with one swing
you said to all of us, this is how it's done. The ball jumps
from your bat over and over. I want my poems to jump
like that. All poems. I want to say once to a world that feels
with reason it has little chance, well done. That's the lie
I cannot shout loud as this local truth: Well done, Mike. Dick.

MANTLE

Mantle ran so hard, they said,
he tore his legs to pieces.
What is this but spirit?

52 homers in '56, the triple crown.
I was a high school junior, batting
fourth behind him in a dream.

I prayed for him to quit, before
his lifetime dropped below .300.
But he didn't, and it did.

He makes Brylcreem commercials now,
models with open mouths draped around him
as they never were in Commerce, Oklahoma,

where the sandy-haired, wide-shouldered boy
stood up against his barn,
lefty for an hour (Ruth, Gehrig),

then righty (DiMaggio),
as his father winged them in,
and the future blew toward him

now a fastball, now a slow
curve hanging
like a model's smile.

FIRST LOVE

Before sixteen
I was fast
enough to fake
my shadow out
and I could read
every crack and ripple
in that catch of asphalt.
I owned
the slanted rim
knew
the dead spot in the backboard.
Always the ball
came back.

Every day I loved
to sharpen
my shooting eye,
waiting
for the touch.
Set shot, jump shot,
layup, hook —
after a while
I could feel
the ball hunger-
ing to clear
the lip of the rim,
the two of us
falling through.

BASKETBALL SEASON BEGINS

Except for the throng
buzzing in the gymnasium,
the town might seem deserted.
Tonight no one drives
up or down Main Street.
Soon every factory worker
balanced on the edge
of the bleachers will
know as exactly as his
boss leaning back in his
chair seat how each of these
high school athletes measures
up against the heroic
individuals on that yardstick
championship team. Every gas
station attendant will be able
to decree as authoritatively
as the superintendent of schools
at what point the new coach's
back deserves to be patted
or his throat summarily slit.
On Monday morning, mayor
and minister alike will inform
their followers exactly why
this team will sputter or soar.
Every native wedged into
this sweaty brick building
has wagered his small town
heritage on the outcome
of this season. The town
has lain dormant for many
a month; at the opening tip-
off it roars itself awake.

SCORING

The pass zaps
from behind a back like a mad electron
blasting free,
crackles to his hand, then,
jabs away at the court,
high bounding and hard.
Possessed, pounding,
he fuses in circuit
to the weird ganglion of
bobbling rubber,
stutter-dribbles, hes-
tates, head fakes,

and breaks,
slicing the stunned circle,
a dazzled filament,
a shard of crystal
splintering clean.
Driving the hoop, he launches,
leaping like energy sizzling
between hot, copper points.

Arched for the lay-up,
sculptured in the detonation
of desire, a glazed arm above
into the stillness,
a touch as soft as fur,
he shoots,
sweeping the volt away,
breaching Zeno's paradox,
crashes to the floor:
forgotten.

Saucy and coy, the ball
jolts a smudgy kiss
on the cold, clear glass,
hangs away on the lip,
moody, weighing the balance,
sighs through the net
like the whisper —
of love.

EDWARD HIRSCH

FAST BREAK

In Memory of Dennis Turner, 1946–1984

A hook shot kisses the rim and
hangs there, helplessly, but doesn't drop,

and for once our gangly starting center
boxes out his man and times his jump

perfectly, gathering the orange leather
from the air like a cherished possession

and spinning around to throw a strike
to the outlet who is already shovelling

an underhand pass toward the other guard
scissoring past a flat-footed defender

who looks stunned and nailed to the floor
in the wrong direction, trying to catch sight

of a high, gliding dribble and a man
letting the play develop in front of him

in slow-motion, almost exactly
like a coach's drawing on the blackboard,

both forwards racing down the court
the way that forwards should, fanning out

and filling the lanes in tandem, moving
together as brothers passing the ball

between them without a dribble, without
a single bounce hitting the hardwood

until the guard finally lunges out
and commits to the wrong man

while the power-forward explodes past them
in a fury, taking the ball into the air

by himself now and laying it gently
against the glass for a lay-up,

but losing his balance in the process,
inexplicably falling, hitting the floor

with a wild, headlong motion
for the game he loved like a country

and swivelling back to see an orange blur
floating perfectly through the net.

DAVID HILTON

I TRY TO TURN IN MY JOCK

*The way I see it, is that when I step out on that court
and feel inside that I can't make the plays,
it'll be time to call it quits.* —Elgin Baylor

Going up for the jump shot,
Giving the kid the head-fakes and all
'Till he's jocked right out the door of the gym
And I'm free at the top with the ball and my touch,
Lofting the arc off my fingertips,
I feel my left calf turn to stone
And my ankle warp inward to form when I land
A neat right angle with my leg,
And I'm on the floor,
A pile of sweat and sick muscles,
Saying,
Hilton,
You're 29, getting fat,
Can't drive to your right anymore,
You can think of better things to do
On Saturday afternoons than be a chump
For a bunch of sophomore third-stringers;
Join the Y, steam and martinis and muscletone.
But, shit,
The shot goes in.

DENNIS TRUDELL

THE JUMP SHOOTER

The way the ball
hung there
against the blue or purple

one night last week
across town
at the playground where

I had gone to spare
my wife
from the mood I'd swallowed

and saw in the dusk
a stranger
shooting baskets a few

years older maybe
thirty-five
and overweight a little

beer belly saw him
shooting there
and joined him didn't

ask or anything simply
went over
picked off a rebound

and hooked it back up
while he
smiled I nodded and for

ten minutes or so we
took turns
taking shots and the thing

is neither of us said
a word
and this fellow who's

too heavy now and slow
to play
for any team still had

the old touch seldom
ever missed
kept moving further out

and finally his t-shirt
a gray
and fuzzy blur I stood

under the rim could
almost hear
a high school cheer

begin and fill a gym
while wooden
bleachers rocked he made

three in a row from
twenty feet
moved back two steps

faked out a patch
of darkness
arched another one and

the way the ball
hung there
against the blue or purple

then suddenly filled
the net
made me wave goodbye

breathe deeply and begin
to whistle
as I walked back home.

WHEN I GOT IT RIGHT

The ball would lift
light as a wish,
gliding like a blessing
over the rim, pure,
or kissing off glass
into the skirt of net.
Once it began
I couldn't miss.
Even in the falling dark,
the ball, before it left
my hand, was sure.

NEW WORLD IN THE MORNING

Somewhere on the outskirts
of a Southeast Texas town
where you burn your neighbor's house
for revenge
and then your own for insurance money
to leave the county,
the Zen Buddhist basketball team
is preparing for its next game.

Friday night on the court,
at peace with themselves,
the fans, the refs, the other players,
they make their baskets every time
and never trip their opponents on fast breaks
or pull their shorts down on jump shots.

Flowing to the rival end of the court
they politely step aside as the Cobras'
star player drives for a layup and,
having nothing to fight for, misses.

Waiting underneath, docile as a doe,
Sardria Char opens his hands
like a baby bird's mouth, open in praise.
Avoiding the karma-disturbing thuds of a dribble,
he takes the ball and hands off to Krishna
who passes to Gandhi sitting cross-legged
and sleepy-eyed under the home town hoop.
The ball rises in a perfect silent curve.
Never touching the rim, it swishes through the net
like a good soul coming into being.

Tonight they subdue with serenity.
Next year they take the title.

TOUCH FOOTBALL

I tackle my father so hard
he fumbles the light
from his frightened hands.
On his back
he looks like a man asleep,
his legs stiff and skinny
in those baggy pants.
              Standing over him
I watch the evening disappear
into his open mouth.
He whispers, "It was only touch."

In high grass I kneel,
touch the small hill behind his ear.
I touch his lips,
blue and dreaming towards the year of his death.
I put on his broken glasses,
stare at the first few stars
breathing above the house.
When the lights come on
I reach into the dark hood of his sweatshirt,
pull it like a dream over his bald head.

It was only touch,
and my father's crooked fingers feel like winter
twisting downriver in the first hush of snow.
I hold his hand tightly on the abandoned field
where this string of losses
still grips our empty hearts, awakened
and unable to forgive.

THE KICKER'S LAST STEPS
—for Jack Driscoll

One point behind, ten seconds left,
I lunge forward

    a halo of gnats around my head.
    I always thought field goal kicking
    should be easy,
    like pushing a word
    from my tongue into the air.
    But the goal posts
    move backward
    ten yards with each step.

    Am I alone on this field—
    only the yard lines like a ladder I've forgotten
    how to climb, the moon's floodlight
    like a stiff graduation gown,
    the empty avenues
    of bleachers?

    When night fog clutches my ankles
    like the pudgy hands of a linebacker,
    I try to think of anything but kicking
    (the river beyond the goal posts,
    the blank scorecards of my parents' faces),
    try not to think that in an instant
    my toe must dive
    deep into leather
    as if it's in love with it.

From the sidelines my approach must look
almost casual, as though I hardly care—
in the silence of this last step
I hear the wings of three ducks above me
flying toward the creaking ice of the river.

DAVID ALLAN EVANS

WATCHING TACKLES IN SLOW MOTION

I key on anything that moves.
    —Deacon Jones

Up floats the turf   the shark is rising
   the slow hawk
               bends the air
tooth and talon
   touch where he moves exactly out of
certain as a polar bear
come from a death
              in the jawed and frozen green
saying
I will always find you   always find you.

scrut gets marty crowe
for social studies

and while his gray voice drones on from the front desk
a slate sky mumps across october windows

the afternoon becomes a cloudy river
begging its way past bending trees

scrut fingers the ragged skin around his knuckles
his eyes catch on a single twisting leaf
tied by last memory of summer
to its branch outside the classroom

> *practice today should be hard as rocks*
> *the cold makes even good hits sting*
> *and crowe that bastard keeps us*
> *out there twice as long*
> *the day before a game*

> *fisting up his face*
> *snapping his cap to the ground*
> *and cracking the raw blue air*
> *with his cursing and roaring*
> *til these eyes water*
> *and these ears ring*

near his window a silent bird
leaps into the bruised air
an empty branch quivers —

> *the real thing quiets him*
> *because we usually win*

> *so friday nights he broods*
> *and paces the sidelines*
> *red face and bullwhip voice hidden*
> *from those in the stands who retell*
> *tales from the practice field and think*
> *they own not only us but him*

the window tilts a quarter inch
and scrut jarred loose from his daydream
lands back inside the classroom

marty crowe is reciting poetry
just as ted heimer said he would

> *the way crowe's voice turns like a leaf in the sun*
> *the way his eyes glaze into a damp middle distance*
> *and float up toward the ceiling*

> *like a man happy to be drowning*

scrut surrenders his breath
to the current of words

the spine of an oak leaf snags on a fallen tree
at a bend in the red cedar river

his football jitters fade then rush out
like a dream on waking and scrut feels
something inside himself break loose

because here is a teacher a teacher
who needs a way out as much as scrut does

and knows it

JAMES WRIGHT

AUTUMN BEGINS IN MARTINS FERRY, OHIO

In the Shreve High football stadium,
I think of Polacks nursing long beers in Tiltonsville,
And gray faces of Negroes in the blast furnace at Benwood,
And the ruptured night watchman of Wheeling Steel,
Dreaming of heroes.

All the proud fathers are ashamed to go home.
Their women cluck like starved pullets,
Dying for love.

Therefore,
Their sons grow suicidally beautiful
At the beginning of October,
And gallop terribly against each other's bodies.

TO BEAR BRYANT,
SOMEWHERE ON THAT TALLER TOWER

In innocence the lines of our palms
are never longer, the blue that the sky
brings to us is always out of our past,
the most important rivers run out of
the smallest glands in our lives.
So much for truths. This morning
the neighbor boy's laughter spraying over
the hedge makes each leaf shine like
a green tongue, while his dog, upside
down, is wriggling his back joyously
into the density of this world. No ideas
but in things, another old coach said.
This morning finds the apple trees
in flower, the sparrows in the gutter,
the big-boned slavic girls, rich
in marrow, on their way to work.
And my neighbor boy with a football
calling his dog in the heaven
of his own backyard. Bear Bryant,
if you're listening, look down.
The way the football flies just so,
in air, like a cardinal between
the red bud and the pear, over the
sensual mouths of the poppies—
look down, Bear Bryant, look down,
once again it's spring practice time,
and the leaves of the dandelions
are speaking long and longer vowels.

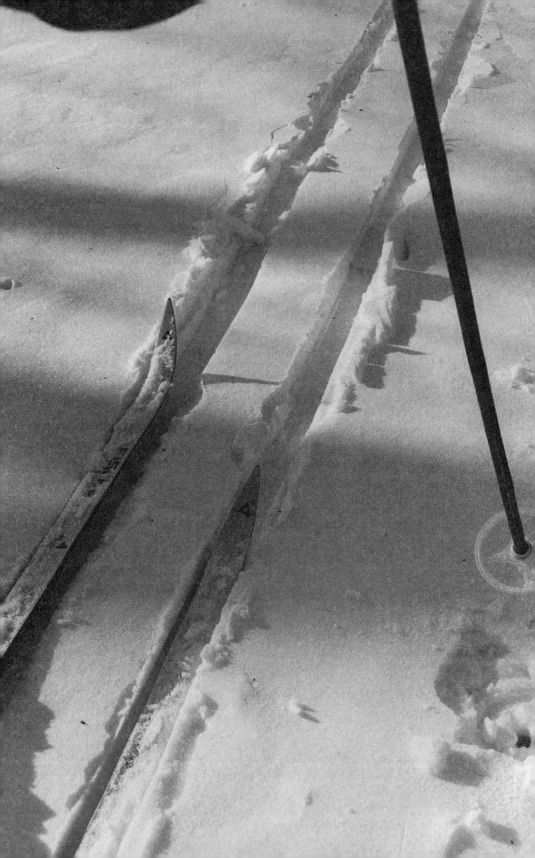

On Incandescent Feet

"Wind is his one competitor"

—Robert Francis, "SKIER"

Elliot Richman

ON THE TOMB OF KALAMACHIUS, THE JOGGER

He slowed once
and death caught him.

DEATH OF THE TRACK STAR

It all happens in a moment, telephone-still.
He leans backward across 30 years in his padded
swivel chair, back toward his high school track.

A magnet pulls at him again
from the finish line, the metal
of his legs is bending, churning.
He feels the choirs of wheezing,
a chestful of cinders.
This is real running, he thinks, his heart
beating hard in his heels.

No one can touch him, yet he touches
everyone: the crowd arches
as he breaks string after string
with his toughened throat and

For an instant he almost believes
he has lived the best possible life—
success pours across the desk in front of him, visible
as spilled coffee. It is the stain
of winning.
He feels a broken glass trophy putting itself
back together again
inside his body. And applause,
like a balloon of light,
surrounds each muscle.

Now his legs can soften into two blue silk ribbons
rippling in the breeze

he smiles, and suddenly inhales
all the breaths
he has ever exhaled in his life.

NIGHT RUNNER'S PRAYER

Tonight I run past the city limit
past the strength of my thighs
carried only by the will to move
out to where the sky reclines
against a brown crust of earth.

Here, undisturbed, a silhouette
against this immense mountain of world,
I watch as the sky, in a dream's liquid motion,
purples the color of desire.

Desire, not as in the want of a man,
the exact antidote to the body's
chemical curiosity, but as in
the desire for access to knowledge of him
past the roots of his sex.

Tonight the sky, black to the east,
wears its purple and orange feathers,
loud and glorious, a canvas of burnt fruit,
the way colors are only where they can't be touched.

But just this once, let gravity unleash me
so that I may run into sky, plum-heavy with rain,
that kingdom more vivid than all my longing.

WILLIAM J. VERNON

OUT ON THE COURSE

On roads, the race drew me outside
myself, running hills, fields and
woodlands, hearing both crow caw and
cow low, fearing that Doberman
growling across a front lawn,
rushing at me in a frenzy.

I was surprised by the beauty,
the sheer shapes of trees bared by fall
and the weather. My hungry eyes saw
it all, the deep ravines where creeks
were washing white rocks, and the steep
slopes were forested as densely
as they'd been in any century.
My cushioned soles felt the impression
of seeds, where corn and wheat had spun
out of combine or picker or loose-boarded

trucks. The homes were sleeping — or emptied
for going to church. A few people
waved from cars. Most stared at the simple,
half-naked men jogging in rain
in the forties, black numbers pinned
to their stomachs. I spoke at one

water stop. A shivering woman
gave me plastic cups. My voice, then,
hadn't worked as well as it should, when
I'd made a joke at twenty miles. My
mouth had stumbled. So I'd tried
again. The words had tripped over
themselves. Cackling, I'd run on, slower.

A JOGGING INJURY

All day I have lain, foot propped,
beating its shadow-heart
in time with the gods who stopped
my run midstride. Their art

stings less in my middle age.
At sixteen I would have cried
at my foot's carnage,
its quick turn from the right.

Now I am riddled with breaks.
Those I loved and others I turned from
have softened my bones to vague aches;
my original dreams come

into my thoughts like dried flowers
too tender for touch. Today blood
crowds and blooms its flower
under the skin, making a glad

try for total repair. The lame
foot struck a rock, innocent
on the path: its pain
is the rock's gift, a godsend.

SKATING AFTER SCHOOL

In the space between school & supper,
light flat as a china plate,
sky and ice a single seam
stitched by the black trees,
we raced over the railroad tracks
down the embankment
to the frozen pond,
mufflers trailing,
snow embroidering our flannel jeans.
Then out, onto the ice, blades dividing
the surface into geometry,
ice writing from an old language,
the calligraphy of snow. . . .
And then, as the baggage of school disappeared,
became ephemeral as smoke from the bonfire
where we charred hot dogs, made dark cocoa
that burned out tongues,
we went back out onto the ice again,
feeling the slap and chock of the hockey puck,
the body contact muffled in layers of wool,
the ache of air inside our lungs. . . .
And as the dark came down like a coffee cup,
we saw the yellow lights come on
up over the tracks.
But we kept on playing, icing the puck,
shooting straight for the goal,
legs aching beyond endurance. . . .
Home, where the yellow lights are growing,
is filling with the smell of macaroni & cheese
and muffins, but we stay out, still checking & hitting
wood against wood, our steel blades marking the ice
until it's a blackboard in need of erasing. . . .
And, when we knew we could not stand it
any longer out in the cold,
we clambered up the banks,
always falling on the cinders,
woodsmoke and winter clinging to our clothes,
climbing, climbing, toward the steady yellow lights of home.

RUTH F. BRIN

ON CEDAR LAKE, 1957

Before our skates had touched the pond that day
We knelt to see, imbedded in the ice,
A fish long dead, his frozen eye turned up;
And further on through surface clear and green
A sluggish waving weed in silent water.
But who could care for all that moved below?
Our skates are sharp, the air is bright,
The lake is wide; we swoop, we glide,
Take flight and dip and swerve
Like gulls. We fly, we fly.

SKATING

Skating on the surface of my life,
I saw myself below the ice,
another me, I was moving fast
above him, he was moving slow,
though he kept up. There must have been
some warp of being twisting
us together so, two different speeds
head to head, or feet to feet, or,
better, shoulder to shoulder, brothers,
that's the way it felt, but separated
by a death, an ice, a long wall
laid down upon the world to lock us
into rooms. Knock, knock. Are you
there? He was, and waving, though
it was a distant wave, an outer-space
wave, as if he were umbilicaled
and drifting off between the stars. The stars
skated on that ice, too, and went so fast
they seemed not to move at all. Perhaps
he was the one sped swerveless home,
an arrow, while I dream-skated,
my two blades, for all their dazzle,
leaving the ice unchanged, and top was
bottom and bottom top, but who could say?
I only knew I wanted to break through.
I wanted the ice to melt to let
us sink together, two lovers in a bed,
or crack, a warning sign missed, while
the stars swam around us like fish
lit up from within by something
we could never name, nor wished to,
lest the light fade. But the ice held,
because it was wiser than I was,
because two is more than twice one,
because the air and water made a pact
to disagree while I skated on
the surface of a life I thought was mine.

SKIER

He swings down like the flourish of a pen
Signing a signature in white on white.

The silence of his skis reciprocates
The silence of the world around him.

Wind is his one competitor
In the cool winding and unwinding down.

On incandescent feet he falls
Unfalling, trailing white foam, white fire.

THE SKIBOMBER

schusssssssss

swoop

— steel

edge/to/ice/edge —

d

o

w   up

n

hanging

over

the world

between outspread arms

below

trees like dark fur

on a small

bear

so

still

closeby gray barkblur

and the distance

still

and clear

clear as a

tink

of ice

across the blue

snow mountain

air

Pursuit

"That either one — or both — or neither one —
Could win?"

—Robert Francis, "Two Wrestlers"

HUNTING FOR GROUSE

It's the yellow time when tamarack sheds.
The evening feeding time, when
trees and rain cut the light
to shreds. There's a woman walking through it.
Past the woman along the creek, a man
walks hidden from her view.

The woman walks and thinks of birds,
how they covey in the brush, flush and fly
before the gun comes up, sometimes whirring
from behind. The woman walks thinking
of birds, not thinking of them. The rain
closing in the woods, the tang of rot.

pungent in the rain, who is the man
calling her? Is it the one who fashioned
rabbit gloves, the one who favors lace—
or one she doesn't know at all? What if she
pulls him down to the leaves and feathers? This
continual calling over the other hill.

Walking stops the voices, The ease
of walking, her hips, the slip
boots make on deadfall in the rain.
Her eyes scan the ground for Kinnikinic,
the split red berries trail the birds to cover.
Twilight brush, mottled gray and brown.

That light on Sundays through yellowed lace.
It was Gramma who did the killing. Her
freckled hands twisted the Banty's neck,
dressed it, trussed it. She took the heart
for gravy. Those tiny bones crackled
under her hands, like underbrush . . .

The bird flies up. The woman stops,
is thinking how a bird's heart is suspended—
a womb between a woman's hips.
She shoots for the head. Waits

'til the eyes cloud over, then
kneels to strip the feathers

to muscle cupped smooth as the upper arm.
He calls to her now, the man who's walking.
His shadow wanders across the filtering
light. The woman looks up—
remembers the one walking with her.
When he steps out to meet her,

she touches the tamarack in his beard.

JACKLIGHT

*The same Chippewa word is used both for flirting and hunting
game, while another Chippewa word connotes both using force in
intercourse and also killing a bear with one's bare hands.*
—R.W. Dunning
Social and Economic Change Among the Northern Ojibwa (1959)

We have come to the edge of the woods,
out of brown grass where we slept, unseen,
out of knotted twigs, out of leaves creaked shut,
out of hiding.

At first the light wavered, glancing over us.
Then it clenched to a fist of light that pointed,
searched out, divided us.
Each took the beams like direct blows the heart answers.
Each of us moved forward alone.

We have come to the edge of the woods,
drawn out of ourselves by this night sun,
this battery of polarized acids,
that outshines the moon.

We smell them behind it
but they are faceless, invisible.
We smell the raw steel of their gun barrels,
mink oil on leather, their tongues of sour barley.
We smell their mothers buried chin-deep in wet dirt.
We smell their fathers with scoured knuckles,
teeth cracked from hot marrow.
We smell their sisters of crushed dogwood, bruised apples,
of fractured cups and concussions of burnt hooks.

We smell their breath steaming lightly behind the jacklight.
We smell the itch underneath the caked guts on their clothes.
We smell their minds like silver hammers

MERLE BASCOM'S .22

"I was twelve when my father gave me this .22
Mossberg carbine — hand-made, with a short octagonal
barrel, stylish as an Indianfighter posing
for a photograph. We ripped up Bokar coffeecans
set into the sandbank by the track — competitive
and companionable. He was a good shot, although
his hands already trembled. Or I walked with my friend
Paul who loved airplanes and wanted to be a pilot,
and carried my rifle loosely, pointing it downward;
I aimed at squirrels and missed. Later I shot woodchucks
that ate my widowed mother's peas and Kentucky
Wonders when I visited on weekends from college,
or drove up from my Boston suburb, finding the gun
in its closet behind the woodstove. Ten years ago
my mother died; I sold up, and moved here with my work
and my second wife, gladly taking my tenancy
in the farmhouse where I intended to live and die.
I used my rifle on another generation
of woodchucks that ate our beans. One autumn an old friend
from college stayed with us after a nervous breakdown:
trembling from electroshock, depressed, suicidal.
I wrapped the octagonal Mossberg in a burlap
bag and concealed it under boards in the old grainshed.
In our quiet house he strengthened and stopped shaking.
When he went home I neglected to retrieve my gun,
and the next summer woodchucks took over the garden.
I let them. Our lives fitted mountain, creek, and hayfield.
Long days like minnows in the pond quickened and were still.
When I looked up from Plutarch another year had passed.
One Sunday the choir at our church sang Whittier's hymn
ending with 'the still small voice of calm.' Idly I thought,
'I must ask them to sing that hymn at my funeral.'
Soon after, I looked for the .22 in the shed,
half expecting it to have vanished, but finding it
wrapped intact where I left it, hardly rusted. I spent
a long evening taking it apart and cleaning it;
I thought of my father's hands shaking as he aimed it.
Then I restored the Mossberg to its accustomed place
in the closet behind the stove. At about this time

I learned that my daughter-in-law was two months pregnant:
It would be the first grandchild. One day I was walking
alone and imagined a granddaughter visiting:
She loved the old place; she swam in the summer pond with us;
she walked with us in red October; she grew older, she fell
in love with a neighbor, she married. . . As I daydreamed,
suddenly I was seized by a fit of revulsion:
I thought: 'Must I go through all that again? Must I live
another twenty years?' It was as if a body
rose from a hole where I had buried it years ago
while my first marriage was twisting and thrashing to death.
One night I was drunk and lost control of my Beetle
off 128 near my ranchhouse. I missed a curve
at seventy miles an hour and careened toward a stone wall.
In a hundredth of a second I knew I would die;
and, as joy fired through my body, I knew something else.
But the car slowed itself on rocks and settled to rest
between an elm and a maple; I sat breathing,
feeling the joy leach out, leaving behind the torment
and terror of my desire. Now I felt this affliction
descend again and metastasize through my body.
Today I drove ninety miles, slowly, seatbelt fastened,
to North Andover and Paul's house, where he lives flying
out of Logan for United. I asked him to hide
the firing pin of an octagonal .22.
He nodded and took it from my hands without speaking.
I cannot throw it away; it was my father's gift."

HUNTING SEASON

One November,
when I was just old enough to ask,
my father was packing his oiled rifles,
red flannels, heavy, woolen socks,
and I wanted to know why he left us
each year to go north to the woods,
sleep in the cold, hugging his Winchester,
waiting for the deer to come.

And I have thought of his answer,
thought of it just the other day
when driving home I saw, in the trunk
of the car in front of me, the head
of a deer, and I knew it was
that season of death again,
that time of leaving.

"Baby," he had said, "there are too many
deer for the slim feedings of the winter fields.
They will starve and die anyway.
This is better, is mercy to the deer."

I believed him, and yet something
in my child's mind resisted this notion
of mercy, resisted the image of my father,
alone on a bright, near-winter morning,
taking aim and spilling blood.

I resist it still, though for fifteen years
my father had rested through this season.
One November, death took him down
with all the hungry and bewildered deer.

But yesterday, while driving west
through a stretch of wood, I saw a doe,
driven by hunger or some strange scent
to the clearing where the highway runs,
and like something human, looked to the road,
and as if she knew no harm would come,
crossed safely over,
and I was glad.

LOUISE ERDRICH

THE STRANGE PEOPLE

> The antelope are strange people. . . they are beautiful to look at, and
> yet they are tricky. We do not trust them. They appear and disappear;
> they are like shadows on the plains. Because of their great beauty, young
> men sometimes follow the antelope and are lost forever. Even if those
> foolish ones find themselves and return, they are never again right in their
> heads.
>
> —Pretty Shield, Medicine Woman of the Crows,
> transcribed and edited by Frank Linderman (1932)

All night I am the doe, breathing
his name in a frozen field,
the small mist of the word
drifting always before me.

And again he has heard it
and I have gone burning
to meet him, the jacklight
fills my eyes with blue fire;
the heart in my chest
explodes like a hot stone.

Then slung like a sack
in the back of his pickup,
I wipe the death scum
from my mouth, sit up laughing,
and shriek in my speeding grave.

Safely shut in the garage,
when he sharpens his knife
and thinks to have me, like that,
I come toward him,
a lean gray witch,
through the bullets that enter and dissolve.

I sit in his house
drinking coffee till dawn,
and leave as frost reddens on hubcaps,
crawling back into my shadowy body.
All day, asleep in clean grasses,
I dream of the one who could really wound me.

STILL HUNTING

Once there were mallards ahead of a blizzard,
their backs to a front of sleet,
and we dug deep into a blind;

and all morning long there were ducks coming in,
maple-leafing down, like the cold fast pitch ı
of breath over our lips.

It was Thanksgiving, a slice of season,
when you looked at my eyes. Young, there must have
been a cold ease about them and a radical vision.

But that was a long time ago. Now among the pintail,
widgeon, wood duck, and scaup, the sun's low,
the wind's tailing down, and the brown phantom

of the evening's first owl's setting sail.
To watch you sluffing along, the breath-frost
in your beard whitening your face,

the stroke you've had
making you do an idiotic dance which you hate
is to watch you lean crookedly against a walking branch.

Gadwall, canvasback, redhead, and teal—
unlocking a gate, you watch the old wire swing back,
slowly catching itself in the cheatgrass.

Over the river the day's last ducks
are penciled chevrons bent in their long, careful arcs.
And pausing, you say, do this for me.

When I'm dead, name things well.
That's all you need of integrity.

ELK CAMP

Everyone else sleeping when I step
to the door of our tent. Overhead,
stars brighter than stars ever were
in my life. And farther away.
The November moon driving
a few dark clouds over the valley.
The Olympic Range beyond.

I believed I could smell the snow that was coming.
Our horses feeding inside
the little rope corral we'd thrown up.
From the side of the hill the sound
of spring water. Our spring water.
Wind passing in the tops of the fir trees.
I'd never smelled a forest before that
night, either. Remembered reading how
Henry Hudson and his sailors smelled
the forests of the New World
from miles out at sea. And then the next thought—
I could gladly live the rest of my life
and never pick up another book.
I looked at my hands in the moonlight
and understood there wasn't a man,
woman, or child I could lift a finger
for that night. I turned back and lay
down then in my sleeping bag.
But my eyes wouldn't close.

The next day I found cougar scat
and elk droppings. But though I rode
a horse all over that country,
up and down hills, through clouds
and along old logging roads,
I never saw an elk. Which was
fine by me. Still, I was ready.
Lost to everyone, a rifle strapped
to my shoulder. I think maybe
I could have killed one.
Would have shot at one, anyway.
Aimed just where I'd been told—

behind the shoulder at the heart
and lungs. "They might run,
but they won't run far.
Look at it this way," my friend said.
"How far would you run with a piece
of lead in your heart?" That depends,
my friend. That depends. But that day
I could have pulled the trigger
on anything. Or not.
Nothing mattered anymore
except getting back to camp
before dark. Wonderful
to live this way! Where nothing
mattered more than anything else.
I saw myself through and through.
And I understood something, too,
as my life flew back to me there in the woods.

And then we packed out. Where the first
thing I did was take a hot bath.
And then reach for this book.
Grow cold and unrelenting once more.
Heartless. Every nerve alert.
Ready to kill, or not.

FISHING

I've got the best seat in the boat
old timers can never resist telling me their secret places
go there, they say, and you're betting big bills
just touch their temples
it all spills out golden silky clear
bout how the water here's just teeming with the big fish
how you just look em in the eye and
they're begging you to fry em for breakfast
rainbow trout is what I'm after
the flashing ones are always the biggest turn on
but findin the right lures
damn hard when you're purblind
those rainbows, slippery bastards
can't hardly touch em from the boat
got to get your legs wet, honey
don't be scared of the water
get out of that skiff
sell yourself damp
those rainbows will be clamoring after your sweet toes
hard against the rocks on the bottom
the water's clean
I wouldn't be here if it wasn't
go ahead now
let em crawl all over you
till your body's rainbow too
pure prism colors
sink down slow and easy
enter water
melt into the great liquid bodies of the north
hidden beauties everywhere
loose limbs
plumb crazy
pears, cherries, berries
the most chilling spring water lake mcdonald has ever put out
put out for me, lake mcdonald
pay me in mountain runoffs

stock the pond for me, fishman
give me streamfed gifts
I can handle rainbows
I give myself up to their tiny bites
know how to return the favor
fishmouth, waterbelly, lilygills, fire-eyes
honey in the water

ROSEANN LLOYD

SONG OF THE FISHERMAN'S LOVER

You stump your way through the tangled
brush, the rocky shore. Listen,
the light in the water
shimmies rainbows across my skin,
the amber sand, my belly
full of roe.

        I know the streams
freeze veins blue as ice,
rocks cut swifter than knives. The chill
you love so well turns gray, turns
glitter. Follow the smell. See
my speckles burn.

        I'll be glassy-eyed
and quick, teasing feathers, the silver
spinners. Nosing every inlet
I'll dance up over the hills and ridges
where waters rush deeper canyons
through white spray to thinner air.

Hurry. The last arch
to the highest waters. Wait madly
for this split suspension
in air. Then head and tail at once
the headfirst dive slaps
thousands of eggs
quivering down.

        Matted and drunk
with honey, you lumber from the brush.
Splash and growl. Say
slime and fur and waters draw
you into me. Dip me from the water.
Kiss the gash. Say *fish.*
Say *woman.*

CRYING UNCLE

1

Uncle Fred never gave up.
He stood out there in the rain all day long,
taking his own sweet time,
casting and reeling in, cold to the bones,
waiting for that old lunker smallmouth to strike.

Twice before, he had hooked Old Beelzebub.
Had felt the line all at once jerk tight
while the rod went crazy and tried to jump in the lake.
Then, when it was already too late,
had witnessed something like fury

come boiling up to the surface,
twisting and thrashing in great fish convulsions,
fighting the thing that dragged it to shore.
In one last leap, it spit out the hook
and fell back to the dark cathedral of water.

The most Uncle Fred ever caught of him
was a shred of ripped lip he kept in a sinker box.
Said if he had to, he'd catch that damn fish
a chunk at a time, put it together
piece by piece like a jigsaw puzzle, by God.

Each time out, before the first cast,
he shook that box to make the lip rattle
and shouted out over the water,
"Here's a hunk of your lip, Old Fish.
Now I've come back for the rest."

2

The last time I saw him alive
was flat on his back between heart attacks
in the Edmore Memorial Hospital.
He pulled at the line that came out of his chest
and begged me to cut him loose.

He reached for his needle-nosed pliers and cried,
"Tommy Boy, there's a hook in my heart,"
and if only I could wiggle it free,
he could head for the drop-off and hide
below the dark, brooding lake.

He thrashed and twisted and cried out in horror
at sheets brown with mud in his bed made of water.
Then his keepers came running and held him down
and pumped him to sleep with morphine.
As he drifted off I watched and waited.

He stared straight through me with shiny fish eyes.
All I could see was the hospital room
and the busy attendants who washed Uncle Fred
and made up the bed he was dying in,
almost as if he weren't there. And maybe he wasn't.

He was out at the lake one last time,
gulping air like a fish out of water,
staring hard at something I couldn't see.
Then he slumped down into his bed and whimpered
and slowly sank out of sight.

CATCH

I imagine us dancing, a Mexican ballroom somewhere
(anything instead of fishing)
In faded, pre-war elegance, tropically flowered wallpaper
(jigs, flies, speckled lures and mr. twisters)
Drooping lushly like the evening sea-breeze
(damn the wind, they won't bite now)
And you in sailor whites—a tuxedo, if I blur my eyes
(black, shiny, slimy leeches, grubs, chubs, fatheads. . .)
The band plays 40's swing, a dark man croons "Darling"
("I'm a rapid oxidizer," you announce, sweat streaming down your nose)
"Darling, Take My Heart. . . "
(walleye, pike, sunstroke, crappies)
And my red dress spins faster as you lift me off the floor
(jesus christ, a four pounder!)
Its ruffled hem streaming round my knees
(landed)
Like a school of tiny iridescent fish
(darling, take my heart)
You sing at last.

PHOTOGRAPH OF MY FATHER
IN HIS TWENTY-SECOND YEAR

October. Here in this dank, unfamiliar kitchen
I study my father's embarrassed young man's face.
Sheepish grin, he holds in one hand a string
Of spiny yellow perch, in the other
A bottle of Carlsbad beer.

In jeans and denim shirt, he leans
Against the front fender of a Ford *circa* 1934.
He would like to pose bluff and hearty for his posterity,
Wear his old hat cocked over his ear, stick out his
tongue. . .
All his life my father wanted to be bold.

But the eyes give him away, and the hands
That limply offer the string of dead perch
And the bottle of beer. Father, I loved you,
Yet how can I say thank you,
    I who cannot hold my liquor either
And do not even know the places to fish?

FISHING THE DREAM

1.

Half asleep
my hand begins to itch
where, hours ago,
I washed the blood from a brook trout
into the river,
and going into the dream,
I felt my hand arc,
tear away,
then circle back,
just above my line of sight,
waiting,
the great fins moving,
the eyes turned slate grey.
This was the beginning of waiting,
imagining the violence of the strike,
the bed moving,
then, limping downstairs,
the house gone icy,
thousands of fishhooks
tangled in the walls.

2.

For a while I stand on one leg
in the current,
letting the other trail off
in front of me,
imagine that it rips away,
then bobs to the surface downstream,
the toes pointed upward,
the calf muscles tight and blue
in the cold water.
In the dream I hobble after it,
and at the pool below Gould's Bend
I watch it glow in the bottom,
the tiny shreds of skin around the edges
waving back in forth in the movement of the river.
For a moment I want to dive down,
pick the stump up in my arms,
bring it to the bank
and try to put it back,
align it bone for bone,
then begin fishing again,
the smell of marrow on my fingers,
my hands holding the line, the rod,
fishing as if my life depended on it.

3.

It comes over and over:
I throw my line out
through the half-mist
hanging like a second skin
over the water,
but it doesn't stop,
just keeps going,
off into the air.
Moments pass,
then minutes.
Nothing.
I poke my rod toward the wall of fog,
hoping for something out there
to take hold,
but it passes through, into nothing.
For an hour I fish the dream,
never sure where my body stops
and the molecules of fog begin.
I sit down on the bank,
try to carve enough space
for my body,
then fold myself into my knees,
knowing that the line is still out there
the hook dragging the stillness.

4.

In 1948, the year I was born,
my father rescued Stan Ash
from the Two-Hearted River
by throwing a monofilament line over him,
waited for his hand to catch,
the line to burrow in
and disappear under the flesh.
Last night I felt that line
cutting into my dream hand,
and when my father pulled me to the surface
the river suddenly widened,
he seemed miles away.

I sat up straight in bed,
ran my finger down through the groove
of my lifeline,
felt the tug of the dream again,
one hand circling in the air,
my father on the bank,
trying to bring me in
so he could cut me free.

TWO WRESTLERS

Two bronzes, but they were passing bronze before
The sculptor

All glint, all gleaming, face to face and grace
To grace

Balanced almost beyond their balance, tingling
To spring —

Who ever saw so point-by-point, so perfect
A pair

That either one — or both — or neither one —
Could win?

If this is trickery, the trick is smooth
In truth

One wrestler challenging — oh how unsafe —
Himself.

BUS DEPOT REUNION

Just over the edge
of my *Life* a young sailor
bounds from a Greyhound's
hiss into his mother's hug,
steps back, trades hands
with his father, then turns
to an old, hunched man
maybe his grandfather —

no hand, no word goes out,
they regard each other,

waiting for something, and
now their hands cup,

they begin to crouch
and spar, the old man

coming on like a pro,
snuffling, weaving,

circling, flicks
out a hook like a lizard's tongue,

the boy ducking, countering,
moving with his moves,

biffing at the bobbing
yellow grin, the clever

head, never landing a real
punch, never taking one

until suddenly, exactly
together they quit,

throw an arm around each other
and walk away laughing

A FIGHTER LEARNS OF HANDS

Hands were not made for hitting.
Learn this and you will know much about hands.
Trace the lines of life in your palm,
Search beyond skin to the constellation of bone
Where the truth about hands is hidden.
Take them outside for a walk
And unglove them in the snow.
Watch them shape the chill air as you
Reach to capture and hold your white breathing.
Close your eyes and place their fingertips
Along the parting of your lips.
Cup them gently against your ears like muffs
and listen to their silence.
You are learning the meaning of hands.

But if in some heated future you forget
And must use them instead for battle,
Must make them into fists and send them against another,
Learn first to fear the hands that hold no memory.
Treat them with suspicion, tape them tighter than a wound
And hide them like a broken secret deep into leather.
Keep the left one near the corner of your eye,
Cock the right one like a cobra at your chin.
Let it strike above the ring. Let it paint the canvas red
Until the final bell lulls you to sleep like a child
Dreaming of stars, until those stars are in your hands,
Until your hands are awake, and beating.

BOXING TOWARDS MY BIRTH

My mother wanted to name me after an Irish thinker:
James Joyce, Sean O'Casey, William Butler Yeats.
But my father thought better of Jack Dempsey,
the "Manassa Mauler." I grew up
shadowboxing with the famous dead.

In the kitchen
my mother read me sad poems that danced for pages
while my father drank himself into the Friday night fights.
Between rounds he stumbled in for bottles of beer,
threw jabs so close to my face
I could feel my first teeth beginning to bleed.
At five I knew words like "knockout," "low blow,"
"straight right."

       That Christmas
I found red boxing gloves under the tree.
They each reminded me of a reindeer's heart
laced tightly around my skinny wrists.
Half naked,
I stood in front of the full length mirror.
My father, smiling, made the sound of a bell
and pushed me closer to the thick glass,
towards the anger of that first punch
I aimed so willingly at myself.

Coaches

" . . . a constellation of players
Shining under his favorite word, *Execution,* . . . "

    —Edward Hirsh, "Execution"

ARCHERY INSTRUCTOR

My boys walk down the range intent to find
Lost arrows well beyond the target flown.
Tomfoolery forgot, they scuff around
The underbrush, each searching on his own.
To them it's treasure hunting of a kind.

But since it's I who am responsible
For all the archery equipment used,
I wait here hoping they will find them all.
The boys move dimly in the woods. Bemused,
I slowly let the scene be blurred unreal

And dream that I might well be Cupid here
Whose orders were: 'Bring back my misfired darts!'
Except on second thought I feel more sure
That what I'd mean is, 'halves of broken hearts.'

A very foolish fond old man, said Lear.

ULYSSES

There is yet some elastic
in this tired old jock,
enough to toss the ball
around and teach my son
Telemachus the subtle art
of looking left — while
thinking right. To catch
the opposition napping,
to cross them up and leave
them guessing. Elastic
yet to flip the pages of
faded clippings and narrate
tales that live as legends:
the hours of practice,
the hard-fought game,
the occasional moments
of glory.

PATRICK WORTH GRAY

NECESSITY IS THE MOTHER OF THE "BULLET"

Our quarterback kept throwing higher
And higher. Finally, the ball
Would just squirt straight up
Thirty yards and straight back
Down into the arms
Of the other team's astonished center.
It was Banana City for Coach Boyle —
"Gray," he said, "Straighten
Rodriguez out." I couldn't speak
Spanish; Rodriguez couldn't speak
English. We drank beer
Until we woke up walleyes
In a recruiting station, signing
The papers. Six months later,
On the slopes of Nui Ba Dinh,
Rodriguez saw a handgrenade
Rolling down toward our hole.
He pitched that thing forty yards
Right into the arms of an eternally
Astonished Viet Cong. After
The echoes died, I said,
"Rodriguez, why the hell didn't you do that
Back at good old P.S.U.?"
"Ah, there," he said, "There, I didn't have to."

136

THE BULL RIDER'S ADVICE

What I'm saying is
you can't take this thing light
and there's no saddle to sit in

you can do it one of two ways
as far as I'm concerned
if you want to do it

you can get on just for the ride
take hold of the rope like it was
any old rope and pray for a quick 8 seconds
and no spinning

or you can wrap your fist into his back
so deep he knows you plan to stay awhile
dig in with your whole soul
until the sonofabitch is sick of you
and lets up

what I'm saying is
it's up to you

EXECUTION

The last time I saw my high school football coach
He had cancer stenciled into his face
Like pencil marks from the sun, like intricate
Drawings on the chalkboard, small x's and o's
That he copied down in a neat numerical hand
Before practice in the morning. By day's end
The board was a spiderweb of options and counters,
Blasts and sweeps, a constellation of players
Shining under his favorite word, *Execution*,
Underlined in the upper right-hand corner of things.
He believed in football like a new religion
And had perfect, unquestioning faith in the fundamentals
Of blocking and tackling, the idea of warfare
Without suffering or death, the concept of teammates
Moving in harmony like the planets — and yet
Our awkward adolescent bodies were always canceling
The flawless beauty of Saturday afternoons in September,
Falling away from the particular grace of autumn,
The clear weather, the ideal game he imagined.
And so he drove us through punishing drills
On weekday afternoons, and doubled our practice time,
And challenged us to hammer him with forearms,
and devised elaborate, last-second plays — a flea-
Flicker, a triple reverse — to save us from defeat.
Almost always they worked. He despised losing
And loved winning more than his own body, maybe even
More than himself. But the last time I saw him
He looked wobbly and stunned by illness,
And I remembered the game in my senior year
When we met a downstate team who loved hitting
More than we did, who battered us all afternoon
With a vengeance, who destroyed us with timing
And power, with deadly, impersonal authority,
Machine-like fury, perfect execution.

FIRST PRACTICE

After the doctor checked to see
we weren't ruptured,
the man with the short cigar took us
under the grade school,
where we went in case of attack
or storm, and said
he was Clifford Hill, he was
a man who believed dogs
ate dogs, he had once killed
for his country, and if
there were any girls present
for them to leave now.
          No one
left. OK, he said, he said I take
that to mean you are hungry
men who hate to lose as much
as I do. OK. Then
he made two lines of us
facing each other,
and across the way, he said,
is the man you hate most
in the world,
and if we are to win
that title I want to see how.
But I don't want to see
any marks when you're dressed,
he said. He said, *Now*.

Playing the Game

"I say, What if I make mistakes as I play?"

—Steve Fortney, "PLAYING SOLITAIRE"

PLAYERS

Early October, maple trees
burning the air. Kirsten
leaned on her rake, said
she was dying. Spoke only once
the Greek names for dying.
She hoarded her words for our game.

Scrabble. Like fiends
every night she was home
we played Scrabble.
Kirsten dazzled the board
with words she had pried
out of doctors, technicians,
made SYZYGY (using two blanks)
and ZYGOT and LYMPH.

Alphabets entered her veins,
dripped letter by letter
through bottles, through tubes.
The score of our games
in her hospital room
was charted like fever.

Home in May. Maple seeds
ticking the screen. Kirsten
spelled BLACK (going across)
and BURY (going down),
made SADLY, made SHADOW,
accused me of letting her win.

Kirsten won, dizzy
with maple seeds falling,
with hundreds and thousands
of words in her cells,
in her veins, with SADLY,
with SHADOW . . .

ARLEEN RUTH COHEN

CHINESE CHECKERS

The dragons
tell me how to move.
like a grasshopper across
the multi colored field
springing from hole to hole
outmaneuvering the beetles.

I see the sacred star
and one by one
I deposit my eggs
until it is
filled and full.

LITTLE GIRL BLUE

Before you know what years are made of they are lost
somewhere down the wooden porch stairs
where your brothers disappear and can hardly be heard
above what must be girls
here we go zoodeeo zoodeeo zoodeeo
here we go zoodeeo all day long
you learn all the words
and hunger the curve of every voice
as you sit among the serious shoes
of Aunt Corinna and Aunt Ida who linger after church
often now that your mother is alone
sometimes they applaud your sweet singing to your dolls
the child takes the nurse the nurse takes the dog
but they never join you down on the scratchy porch rug
the way your mother does
but then you do not remember when she disappears
behind the screen door at the top of the stairs
and you are standing at the edge
your desire a perfect swoop and soar of the game
the big girls play
but the big girls never believe you
and you do not know this for many years
because they smile and close their hands and do not let you
escape the strong brown circle
red rover red rover I call Evangeline over
now you are redlightgreenlight quick
now you are polite *mother may I? take two giant steps*
backwards yes you may
no they never believe
engine engine #9 going down Chicago line
you come too late
if the train goes off the track do you want your money back?
and leave too soon
you pick up all the sticks
you pick up all the jacks one by one
you are a safety-first player you are a gambler
but you do not know it now
all these years when your opponent is unknown
the cheese stands alone

MICHAEL CLEARY

AFTER READING THE GREAT AMERICAN MARBLE BOOK AND REFLECTING ON LIFE'S LESSONS LEARNED AT AN EARLY AGE IN GLENS FALLS, N.Y.

1. *Negotiate*

    Ring Taw? Ringer? Chasies?
    Boss-Out, Bullseye, Puggy?
    Zulu Golf?

2. *Know the Rules*

    Dubs and Snoogers.
    Lagging, Throwsies,
    Eye Drops, Toe-Bombsies.
    Monkey Dust. Double Monkey Dust.
    Knuckle Down, Three-Finger Flat:
    firing, flicking, pinching,
    dribbling, drizzying, pinking.
    No Histing or Fudging;
    no Cunny Thumb, no Slipsies;
    no Scrumpy Knuckles
    or Hunching.

3. *Ante Up*

    Ducks:
    Cats Eyes, Clayeys, Candy Stripes.
    Peewees, Purees, Smokeys.
    Mibs, Milkies, Moonaggies.
    Clodknockers. Globollas. Hoodles.
    Marididdles.

4. *Seize the Initiative*

    Shooters:
    Boss, Black Beauty.
    Kabola, Boulder,
    Bumboozer.
    Steelie, Zebra,
    Rainbow Reeler.

5. *Learn from Experience*

    Playing for Fun
    's not worth playing at all.

BARBARA GOLDOWSKY

PLAYING THE GAME

You stick out your fist: *stone*
breaks my two fingers playing *scissors*.

You offer your hand, open.
I shred the palm: it's *paper*.
I am still *scissors*.

Have you no heart? you ask.
But I am *stone*.

Your hand is still *paper*,
you wrap me up:
closer than blades,
harder than hearts.

Theresa Pappas

PLAYING TIME

On the front steps, our mothers wait for us, flushed
in their pastels and bermuda shorts. Our jump
ropes have coiled to the ground, chalk margins dissolved
on the avenue. It's getting dark as we lean
back on their sunburned knees, while they talk as though
we aren't there about the note Irene left her
husband, the hole Jim put in the bedroom wall
with his fist, and how thirteen year old Betty
teases her hair now. Then they teach us a game
called Time. The mothers nod and touch our shoulders
to tell us where to sit. They ask questions
and range us on the steps by our answers. Joy and
Janie answer, take new places, answer, brush
against me as they move again. The questions
are hard: I finally lose each step I gain.
The game can't end. We play Time for hours. I wait
for my turn and follow the croon of questions,
the signals to move, the mild halt of a wrong
answer, the penalty of descent. Passing
cars brighten the asphalt briefly, the rub of
tires erasing for a moment the sounds of
crickets and cars down on Belair Road. It's dark
now. I can't see the scoop of freckles on my
mother's neck, so I look through the trees for a
simple constellation, something I would know.
I listen for my own mother's voice. She speaks
tonight without the strain of calling me, as
she must each day to span the neighborhood with
the syllables of my name, calling me to
lunch and supper, chores and sleep, calling me away
from other games. This time I want to answer.

SYMA CHERIS COHN

THE YO-YO KING

When he showed up on the sidewalk in the old neighborhood, the children gathered around him. At the top of an incline he stood, his black hair glistening, the lavender yo-yo spinning. With pressed black pants and white shirt, he was willing to play games. He could make a yo-yo walk, sleep and rock the baby, then snap it back. He proposed contests. He gave glittering yo-yos and singing strings as prizes.

Was he sent by the company, all the way from the Orient?

It cost 50 cents for a fairly good Duncan, shiny and black. The lavender model with rhinestones was $2.50. Nobody had that kind of money. Most of us bought the dull, red and black twenty-five-centers.

We tried to make our yo-yos do his tricks. We practiced. We bought new strings, believing the secret was in the strings. We dreamed we could make our yo-yos dance.

We waited for the king to return. After long intervals, new kings would appear. Never the same king. We put our yo-yos in a drawer. We played jacks. We played ball. We went to school. And slowly we forgot.

PLAYING SOLITAIRE

My teacher and I sit down.
I put the deck between us.

I say, Go ahead.

Well, he says (as one who sees
everything), if you play that
deck and use the 7 across
1 at a time method,
you will lose the game.
If you use the 7 across
3 at a time, you will lose,
but have 10 cards
on aces above the deck.
If you use the 7 across
3 at a time method
with the Cummings shuffle
you will still lose
but have 27 cards
on aces above the deck.

I say, What if I make mistakes as I play?

I've already figured all that in.

But then what if *you* make the mistake in the deal?

I told you I've figured *all* the errors in!

Now shuffle the cards again.

With that deck. . . .

JUDITH EMLYN JOHNSON

ARGUMENT ONE: THE LADY SHEWS HOW SHE IS FORSAKEN FOR A PIECE OF WOOD

Now, put me near your chess
pieces, the Queen, near Her /
see how She surpasses me
point for point, body, soul / Her very line
being both straight and lean
contains more grace than mine
and royal, She claims total loyalty. Her mind
is sharper than my human
mind because it's confined
in a many-pointed crown, and hard
the center through. Her eyes see equally
all ways at once, nor can Her heart be ruled
by sight slipped through Her guard
to shake Her to joy or tears,
nor Her face shocked to show what Time has tooled
with patient, cutting years
or Chance has brought to bear
with pressure, for Her face looks everywhere,
selfwilled as they must be who mock surprise.
       She moves as She will
no farther than She will
and just as far, and east and west the same /
direction has no name
to Her / She is the compass and the winds.

how tell Her that though
i move one way and one alone and see
one line at a time to keep to, i have what
She lacks the wit to know She lacks. Time
will take Her, She must lose,
be locked in a box like me
but must return to Her central
throne each game /
She moves not up nor down
but sideways / though She hold all
directions in Her crown
She has not power to climb
heaven / love, She has not power to fall
as far as hell when you put Her down, can't feel
how Her game ends
        while mine goes on
        as long as flesh will tell.

A WORLD WAR II PREMIUM FROM BATTLE CREEK

Breakfast more than he could want,
he eats quickly every morning, takes seconds
to empty the Kellogg's cereal box
and knife out the enemy on the back.

Printed on PEP! box backs, three ways:
Hitler is black dots and brown
swung in a scowl, his mustache
a broken piece of pocket comb,
mouth slashed red dots in the brown.

Sides of riboflavin, thiamine,
but on the backs adrenaline:
Mussolini, mostly jaw, confetti dots of red
and two day whiskers sprinkled black
like Sunday comics magnified.

On each scowling Axis face,
concentric targets printed red-white-blue
so he can aim and score
the pocket knife or rock.

Tojo is all dark yellow dots, except
for the buck-toothed white, and spidery
glasses outlined in black,

the boy's kindergarten favorite,
but Mr. Seigel at the Southside Store
hardly ever has Tojo in stock,
he's overstocked with Hitler.

A rock on the nose is a bullseye,
a hundred points. The boy prefers the eyes.
Tacked to the backyard tree, the cardboard skin
tears with a jagged rock but
will not bleed, and Tojo's glasses never break.

This Sporting Life

". . . the single body, alone in the universe . . . "

—Sharon Olds, "SEX WITHOUT LOVE"

LOUISVILLE FEARED IN MIDEAST

after a newspaper headline

You can't buy baseball bats in Israel
You can't bring them in, either
(The batting gloves tucked in your belt give you away)
God forbid you could poke somebody's eye out
Louisville feared in Mideast

You can't make crime pay in Egypt
Egyptian justice will track you down
Your cell has no windows, no telephone, no *Reader's Digest*
They turn on the TV
NCAA basketball playoffs
Louisville feared in Mideast

You can't predict the price of oil
With the tools of supply and demand
The Arab oil ministers use their own tools
"And in today's results
Chiropractor ran last in the fourth
While Stormin' Norman failed to show."
Louisville feared in Mideast

THE ANNOUNCER

Makes up the game
as he goes along
is all the heroes
who slug homers or
steal home

acts as if
he doesn't know
the outcome
but of course
he does, plays dumb

done, dumps
fans and players and umps
into his pockets
folds up the stadium
shuts off his mouth

LAST GAME

Today your old golf clubs arrived
with your ghost at my front door.
I saw the date of the last game
you ever played stamped in pale red
on the ticket tied to the strap.
I saw how you must have hoisted the bag
over your shoulder, setting out tired
and by then not loving it much.
The ticket says: 18 Holes, South Pine Creek Park.
It warns: Always keep in sight.
And: Good only on the date issued.

My son finds in a pocket of the bag
a bandaid you kept for blisters
and a split black driving glove,
such very small things.
Nothing could protect you by then,
the truth of sun in your eyes,
the trees staggering farther and farther away
as you stepped off the green.

What kind of day was it?
I want to think a white gauze cloud day,
a few birds, you out there alone,
and the ball going where you wanted it to go.
My son says he has never seen a sand wedge,
studies it, rubs its grain, its chip marks.
He knows this is the club for difficult places,
for the ball that will elude you,
your strokes slipping down between grains of sand.

SPIEL

Touching the leg of a girl
I used to go to bed with,
I was waiting for something
to happen, something
unusual, or more promising.
What did it matter that I had no eye
for her, or anyone else for that matter?
We'd tried various things for breakfast
but breakfast remained our most
uninteresting meal of the day.
Stormclouds appeared on the horizon,
just letting us know that Nature
has the final say in things,
and then they went away.
In the early afternoon, a softball game
formed on the playing field. A batsman
with a level swing popped one up high
to the infield. All eyes were on the ball
as it neared the zenith of its arc,
but then to our amazement, instead of falling,
it arched even higher, looped the loop,
and, gathering speed and swelling, flew into
orbit around the earth. There it glides
to this day, a second moon, and people say,
"How lovely it is. Both moons are out tonight."

MISS SUMMERFEST

First, the mandatory poses:
double arm front,
quarter turn to the left
side tricep,
back spread,
double arm, back on toes
down,
another quarter turn,
side tricep,
side chest, to the front
front lat spread,
your most muscular pose,
extend right leg and flex,
extend left leg and flex.

The judges
the judges are
not unanimous, but
majority rules:
five-foot-eight-inch Sherie Stevacki,
who has only been training for six months,
wins best poser;
Tina Louise wins most muscular.
But it's Melody Peach the big prize winner,
Miss Summerfest, she walks off with her trophy.
Everyone is laughing: they put a man on top
the woman winner's trophy.
She'll have more fun with him anyway,
yells the drunk in the back.
And Melody, why Melody Peach
just swings that three-foot trophy home
like a baby to her breast.
She slides her baby-oiled, brown-skinned
bottle-green-bikinied body off the stage
sways
like she was going to show her lats all over again,
winks and is gone.

A Melody you'll never know the words to
is the joke in more than one mind.
If Melody were a place
she wouldn't be named yet;
she wouldn't even be discovered
except maybe in the dark
of Lafcadio Hearn's blind eye
in one of his dreams
on one of his hungry nights in New Orleans.

The rest of us just wish that place
in deep sleeps and waitings mostly
too deep to remember

Melody's gone,
her well-oiled feet
left footprints in
the dusty hearts of many
in the dusty fairgrounds crowd.

THE ROAN HUNTER

Again she learns to move
to the trot, to the question, why
did she let this language
fall out of use? not

A profession for a girl,
better to read *Reader's Digest*
condensed novels, safer
than the strong flesh, the

Neck crest, better. . .
better not, the wounds
of the past red as her
roan hunter's fire tail

Loping across Back Brook
across Mulhockaway Creek
the horse stops to drink,
to trail snatch, she

Rides backwards into
memory, a wall
of blue ribbons
in spite of: later is when

You get what you want, sit
trot, sit trot three
strides down the diagonal
change rein, pushing

The horse forward with
her calves, with the balance
of her weight, her hands
light on the bit, a calling

A voice she had
to shut out, no place
for a girl moving up
sordid rooms and sordid

Men, horse traders, race
track talk and double talk
—would pay you what I
owe, but—the roan hunter,

Did they know what they
were taking away? more than
a thousand pounds of muscle from
a girl alone on the trail where

Even men with guns and dogs
are afraid of a woman
on a horse, —"she spent
every hour riding, so we

Weaned her, took her
privileges away"—, took
away the horse girl hired out
at the State Fair,

The High Jump, over
a stone wall sideways as
all the rodeo cowboys
cheered, what we lose

When we move up, not just
the rhythm of hooves
on the frozen ground, but
a meter beating

Forever in her heart
her fingers tapping
the typewriter to a voice
denied, now she speaks

So well the language
of her station, her mouth
moves in precision,
a dressage drill, words

Dressed in top hats and tails
in white breeches, white
gloved words in black
boots, her words fingered

Gently like the reins,
like blood pulsing to
the noise of hooves
on a mud slick road

Her blood speaks the language
of horses, and it
all comes back, it
all comes back

MY BOAT

My boat is being made to order. Right now it's about to leave
the hands of its builders. I've reserved a special place
for it down at the marina. It's going to have plenty of room
on it for all my friends: Richard, Bill, Chuck, Toby, Jim, Hayden,
Gary, George, Harold, Don, Dick, Scott, Geoffrey, Jack,
Paul, Jay, Morris, and Alfredo. All my friends! They know who
    they are.
Tess, of course. I wouldn't go anyplace without her.
And Kristina, Merry, Catherine, Diane, Sally, Annick, Pat,
    Judith, Susie, Lynne, Cindy, Jean, Mona.
Doug and Amy! They're family, but they're also my friends,
and they like a good time. There's room on my boat
for just about everyone. I'm serious about this!
There'll be a place on board for everyone's stories.
My own, but also the ones belonging to my friends.
Short stories, and the ones that go on and on. The true
and the made-up. The ones already finished, and the ones still
    being written.
Poems, too! Lyric poems, and the longer, darker narratives.
For my painter friends, paints and canvases will be on board
    my boat.
We'll have fried chicken, lunch meats, cheeses, rolls,
French bread. Every good thing that my friends and I like.
And a big basket of fruit, in case anyone wants fruit.
In case anyone wants to say he or she ate an apple,
or some grapes, on my boat. Whatever my friends want,
name it, and it'll be there. Soda pop of all kinds.
Beer and wine, sure. No one will be denied anything, on
    my boat.
We'll go out into the sunny harbor and have fun, that's the idea.
Just have a good time all around. Not thinking
about this or that or getting ahead or falling behind.
Fishing poles if anyone wants to fish. The fish are out there!
We may even go a little way down the coast, on my boat.
But nothing dangerous, nothing too serious.
The idea is simply to enjoy ourselves and not get scared.
We'll eat and drink and laugh a lot, on my boat.
I've always wanted to take at least one trip like this,

with my friends, on my boat. If we want to
we'll listen to Schumann on the CBC.
But if that doesn't work out, okay,
we'll switch to KRAB, The Who, and the Rolling Stones.
Whatever makes my friends happy! Maybe everyone
will have their own radio, on my boat. In any case,
we're going to have a big time. People are going to have fun,
and do what they want to do, on my boat.

A JOCKEY

named Kovacs went down
at Pomona yesterday.
He was riding something
that was born to hold
one piece of paper
to another.

The crowd loves to hate
accidents and everybody
wanted to know who Ted
Kovacs was. Like the
next winner, it was
a mystery.

This, then, is to set
the record straight:
Ted Kovacs makes 14
thousand a year when
things go right.

His wife keeps a
scrapbook that shows
the day he tripled,
the $9000.00 Exacta
where he was second,
and all the times he
was in intensive care.

When he almost didn't make it,
the article ran to nearly
20 lines.

Robert Bly

THE HOCKEY POEM
for Bill Duffy

1. The Goalie

The Boston College team has gold helmets, under which the long black hair of the Roman centurion curls out. . . . And they begin. How weird the goalies look with their African masks! The goalie is so lonely anyway, guarding a basket with nothing in it, his wide lower legs wide as ducks'. . . . No matter what gift he is given, he always rejects it. . . . He has a number like 1, a name like Mrazek, sometimes wobbling his legs waiting for the puck, or curling up like a baby in the womb to hold it, staying a second too long on the ice.

The goalie has gone out to mid-ice, and now he sails sadly back to his own box, slowly; he looks prehistoric with his rhinoceros legs; he looks as if he's going to become extinct, and he's just taking his time. . . .

When the players are at the other end, he begins sadly sweeping the ice in front of his house; he is the old witch in the woods, waiting for the children to come home.

2. The Attack

They all come hurrying back toward us, suddenly, knees dipping like oil wells; they rush toward us wildly, fins waving, they are pike swimming toward us, their gill fins expanding like the breasts of opera singers; no, they are twelve hands practicing penmanship on the same piece of paper. . . . They flee down the court toward us like birds, swirling two and two, hawks hurrying for the mouse, hurrying down wind valleys, swirling back and forth like amoebae on the pale slide, as they sail in the absolute freedom of water and the body, untroubled by the troubled mind, only the body, with wings as if there were no grave, no gravity, only the birds sailing over the cottage far in the deep woods. . . .

Now the goalie is desperate. . . he looks wildly over his left shoulder, rushing toward the other side of his cave, like a mother hawk whose chicks are being taken by two snakes. . . suddenly he flops on the ice like a man trying to cover a whole double bed. He has the puck. He stands up, turns to his right, and drops it on the ice at the right moment; he saves it for one of his children, a mother hen picking up a seed and then dropping it. . .

But the men are all too clumsy, they can't keep track of the puck. . . no, it is the *puck*, the puck is too fast, too fast for human

168

beings, it humiliates them. The players are like country boys at the fair watching the con man—the puck always turns up under the wrong walnut shell. . . .

They come down ice again, one man guiding the puck this time. . . and Ledingham comes down beautifully, like the canoe through white water, or the lover going upstream, every stroke right, like the stallion galloping up the valley surrounded by his mares and colts, how beautiful, like the body and soul crossing in a poem. . . .

3. Trouble

The player in position pauses, aims, pauses, cracks his stick on the ice, and a cry as the puck goes in! The goalie stands up disgusted, and throws the puck out. . . .

The player with a broken stick hovers near the cage. When the play shifts, he skates over to his locked-in teammates, who look like a nest of bristling owls, owl babies, and they hold out a stick to him. . . .

Then the players crash together, their hockey sticks raised like lobster claws. They fight with slow motions, as if undersea. . . they are fighting over some tribal insult or a god, but like lobsters they forget what they're battling for; the clack of the armor plate distracts them, and they feel a pure rage.

Or a fighter sails over to the penalty box, where ten-year-old boys wait, to sit with the criminal, who is their hero. . . . They know society is wrong, the wardens are wrong, the judges hate individuality. . . .

4. The Goalie

And this man with his peaked mask, with slits, how fantastic he is, like a white insect, who has given up on evolution in this life; his family hopes to evolve after death, in the grave. He is ominous as a Dark Ages knight. . . the Black Prince. His enemies defeated him in the day, but every one of them died in their beds that night. . . . At his father's funeral, he carried his own head under his arm.

He is the old woman in the shoe, whose house is never clean, no matter what she does. Perhaps this goalie is not a man at all, but a woman, all women; in her cage everything disappears in the end; we all long for it. All these movements on the ice will end, the

advertisements come down, the stadium walls bare. . . . This goalie
with his mask is a woman weeping over the children of men, that are
cut down like grass, gulls that stand with cold feet on the ice. . . .
And at the end, she is still waiting, brushing away the leaves, waiting
for the new children developed by speed, by war. . . .

PASSAGE RITE

They call them Wet and Dry,
two abandoned pits concealed in woods and hills
south of town, hard enough to get to,
far enough to be worthy for a rite.
The path ducks through tilted concrete piers
and the huge rusted bones of mining machines.

Two dug holes a hundred yards across and deep,
exhausted of iron and long left to boys, between them
only a bridge of land at its widest the width
of outstretched ten-year-old hands.

Wet is a giant's version of that Mayan sacrifice well,
quarried red walls leading the eye down
to water cold and paintrock red and calm,
without a ledge to crawl out on.
Where a kid was supposed to have drowned.

And Dry, a mountain cirque closed off,
cliffed and gullied, steep fans of taconite scree,
bits of moss green scattered down the sides
where groundwater seeps, and on the floor
the thread of a stream, a clump of alder scrub.
As deep, but a somehow more attractive fall.

So the boy comes to the ritual bridge,
as all the Southside boys do in their time,
to try the narrow rock and gravel path.
Small rockslides down the widening sides,
and all muscles taut across and back.

He walks barefoot and he walks alone,
without touching fingers to the ground.
A few bad places where he wants hands and knees,
where a loose pebble or a sudden wish
can make him choose between Wet and Dry.

He knows nothing of why. The ancient choice
is dared, and he learns the passage of Wet and Dry,

learns more than the fear his flesh sings.
Somewhere on that sliding edge he finds
the wish to be undone, that wish as soon erased
as he gains the trees and waiting hands.

The boy does not know he will walk that narrow path
for years. Each time he does not belong,
he will hear the falling rocks behind his feet,
and inch across the night between two ways to die.

SEX WITHOUT LOVE

How do they do it, the ones who make love
without love? Beautiful as dancers,
gliding over each other like ice-skaters
over the ice, fingers hooked
inside each other's bodies, faces
red as steak, wine, wet as the
children at birth whose mothers are going to
give them away. How do they come to the
come to the   come to the   God   come to the
still waters, and not love
the one who came there with them, light
rising slowly as steam off their joined
skin? These are the true religious,
the purists, the pros, the ones who will not
accept a false Messiah, love the
priest instead of the God. They do not
mistake the lover for their own pleasure,
they are like great runners: they know they are alone
with the road surface, the cold, the wind,
the fit of their shoes, their over-all cardio-
vascular health—just factors, like the partner
in the bed, and not the truth, which is the
single body alone in the universe
against its own best time.

ACKNOWLEDGMENTS

We gratefully acknowledge permission to reprint materials from the following sources:

Robert Bly, "The Hockey Poem," from *The Morning Glory* (Harper and Row, 1975). Copyright © by Robert Bly. Reprinted by permission of the author.

Michael Dennis Browne, "Handicapped Children Swimming," first published in *The New Yorker* and later in *The Wife of Winter* (Charles Scribner's Sons, 1970). Copyright © by Michael Dennis Browne. Reprinted by permission of the author.

Kent Cartwright, "Scoring," in *Arete: The Journal of Sport Literature*, vol. 1, no. 2 (spring 1984). Copyright © by Kent Cartwright. Reprinted by permission of the author.

Raymond Carver, "Elk Camp" and "My Boat," from *Where Water Comes Together with Other Water* (Random House, 1984, 1985). Copyright © by Raymond Carver. Reprinted by permission of the author. "Photograph of My Father in His Twenty-Second Year," from *Fires*. Copyright © 1983 by Raymond Carver. Reprinted by permission of Capra Press.

Michael Cleary, "After Reading *The Great American Marble Book* and Reflecting on Life's Lessons Learned at an Early Age in Glens Falls, N.Y.," in *Sunrust* (fall 1984). Copyright © by Michael Cleary. Reprinted by permission of the author.

Arleen Ruth Cohen, "Chinese Checkers," in *Newsletter Inago*, vol. 6, no. 4 (April 1986). Copyright © by Arleen Cohen. Reprinted by permission of the author.

Barbara Crooker, "Deliverance," in *Festival*, vol. 3 (May 1979). "Skating after School," in *West Branch*, no. 17 (1985). Copyright © by Barbara Crooker. Reprinted by permission of the author.

Philip Dacey, "Mystery Baseball," from *The Boy Under the Bed*. Copyright © 1981 by Philip Dacey. Reprinted by permission of the Johns Hopkins University Press. "Skating," from *The Man with the Red Suspenders* (Milkweed Editions, 1986). Copyright © by Philip Dacey. Reprinted by permission of the author.

Alixa Doom, "Snorkeling in the Caribbean," in *Lake Street Review*, no. 19, (summer 1985). Copyright © by Alixa Doom. Reprinted by permission of the author.

Jack Driscoll, "Boxing Towards My Birth" and "Touch Football," from *Fishing the Backwash* (Ithaca House, 1984). Copyright © by Jack Driscoll. Reprinted by permission of the author.

Louise Erdrich, "Jacklight" and "The Strange People," first published in *Frontiers* and later in *Jacklight* (Holt, Rinehart and Winston, 1984). Copyright © by Louise Erdrich. Reprinted by permission of the author.

David Allan Evans, "Bus Depot Reunion" and "The Bull Rider's Advice," in *Shenandoah*, vol. 25, no. 2 (1974). "Watching Tackles in Slow Motion," in *Shenandoah*, vol. 21, no. 1, (1979). Copyright © 1974/1979 by Washington and Lee University. "Pole Vaulter," in *Esquire* (November 1972). Copyright © by David Allan Evans. Reprinted by permission of the author.

Robert Francis, "Skier," from *Robert Francis: Collected Poems, 1936–1976* (Amherst: University of Massachusetts Press, 1976). Copyright © 1959 by Robert Francis. Reprinted by permission. "The Base Stealer" © 1948, "Swimmer" © 1953, "Two Wrestlers" © 1959. All from *The Orb Weaver*. Copyright © 1960 by Robert Francis and Wesleyan University Press. Reprinted by permission of University Press of New England.

Norman German, "New World in the Morning," in *The Worcester Review*, vol. 8, no. 2 (fall 1985). Copyright © by Norman German. Reprinted by permission of the author.

Charles Ghigna, "Divers," in *Southern Poetry Review*, vol. 16 (1977). Copyright © by Charles Ghigna. Reprinted by permission of the author. "A Fighter Learns of Hands," in *Arete: The Journal of Sport Literature*, vol. 2, no. 2 (spring 1985). Copyright © by Charles Ghigna. Reprinted by permission of the author.

Gary Gildner, "First Practice," from *First Practice*. Copyright © 1969 by the University of Pittsburgh Press. Reprinted by permission of the University of Pittsburgh Press. "In My Meanest Daydream," from *Clackamas* (Carnegie Mellon University Press, 1991). Copyright © by Gary Gildner. Reprinted by permission of the author.

Patricia Goedicke, "In the Ocean," from *Crossing the Same River* (Amherst: The University of Massachusetts Press, 1980). Copyright © by The University of Massachusetts Press. Reprinted by permission of The University of Massachusetts Press.

Patrick Worth Gray, "Necessity Is the Mother of the 'Bullet'," first published in *Mojo Navigator(e)*, no. 5 (1976), and later reprinted in *Vietnam Flashbacks* (Pig Iron Press, 1984). Copyright © by Patrick Worth Gray. Reprinted by permission of the author.

Donald Hall, "Couplet" and "Merle Bascom's .22," from *The Happy Man*. Copyright © 1981, 1982, 1983, 1984, 1985, 1986 by Donald Hall. Reprinted by permission of Random House, Inc.

Tom Hansen, "Crying Uncle," in *Poetry Northwest*, vol. 15, no. 4 (winter 1984–85). Copyright © by Tom Hansen. Reprinted by permission of the author.

William Heyen, "Mantle," from *The Host: Selected Poems 1965–1990*. Reprinted by permission of Time Being Books. Copyright © 1994 by Time Being Press. All rights reserved.

David Hilton, "I Try to Turn in My Jock," from *Huladance*. Copyright © 1976 by David Hilton. Reprinted by permission of Crossing Press.

Edward Hirsch, "Fast Break," from *Wild Gratitude*. Copyright © 1985 by Edward Hirsch. Reprinted by permission of Alfred A. Knopf. "Execution," from *The Night Parade*. Copyright © 1989 by Edward Hirsch. Reprinted by permission of Alfred A. Knopf.

Richard Hugo, "Missoula Softball Tournament." Copyright © 1973 by Richard Hugo. "Letter to Mantsch from Havre." Copyright © 1977 by W. W. Norton. Both from *Making Certain It Goes On: The Collected Poems of Richard Hugo*. Reprinted by permission of W. W. Norton and Company, Inc.

Fleda Brown Jackson, "A Jogging Injury," *Windless Orchard*, no. 46, (fall 1985). Copyright © by Fleda Brown Jackson. Reprinted by permission of the author.

Halvard Johnson, "Americans Playing Slow-Pitch Softball at an Airbase near Kunsan, South Korea," in *The Asian Marylander*, no. 7 (spring/summer 1981). Copyright © by Halvard Johnson. Reprinted by permission of the author. "The Extra-Inning Ballgame," from *The Dance of the Red Swan*. Copyright © 1971 by Halvard Johnson. Reprinted by permission of New Rivers Press.

Judith Emlyn Johnson, "Argument One: The Lady Shews How She Is Forsaken for a Piece of Wood," from *Town Scold* (Countryman, 1977). Copyright © by Judith Emlyn Johnson. Reprinted by permission of the author.

Galway Kinnell, "On the Tennis Court at Night," from *Mortal Acts, Mortal Words*. Copyright © 1980 by Galway Kinnell. Reprinted by permission of Houghton Mifflin Co. All rights reserved. Republished in *Three Books* (1993).

Emilie Buchwald is the cofounder, publisher, and editor of *Milkweed Editions,* and the author of two prize-winning children's novels.

Ruth Roston is the author of *I Live in the Watchmaker's Town* (New Rivers Press) and coeditor of *Mixed Voices* and *The Poet Dreaming in the Artist's House* (both Milkweed Editions). Her poems have appeared in a number of journals and anthologies, including *Minnesota Writes: Poetry* (Milkweed Editions).

AUTHORS/*THIS SPORTING LIFE*

Interior design by Randy Scholes
Typeset in Bembo
by Stanton Publication Services, Inc.
Printed on acid-free 55# Booktext Natural paper
by BookCrafters

More poetry anthologies from Milkweed Editions:

Clay and Star:
Contemporary Bulgarian Poets
Translated and edited
by Lisa Sapinkopf and Georgi Belev

Drive, They Said:
Poems about Americans and Their Cars
Edited by Kurt Brown

Looking for Home:
Women Writing about Exile
Edited by Deborah Keenan and Roseann Lloyd

Minnesota Writes:
Poetry
Edited by Jim Moore and Cary Waterman

Mixed Voices:
Contemporary Poems about Music
Edited by Emilie Buchwald and Ruth Roston

Mouth to Mouth:
Poems by Twelve Contemporary Mexican Women
Edited by Forrest Gander

Night Out:
Poems about Hotels, Motels, Restaurants, and Bars
Edited by Kurt Brown and Laure-Anne Bosselaar

Passages North Anthology:
A Decade of Good Writing
Edited by Elinor Benedict

The Poet Dreaming in the Artist's House:
Contemporary Poems about the Visual Arts
Edited by Emilie Buchwald and Ruth Roston

This Sporting Life:
Contemporary American Poems
about Sports and Games
Edited by Emilie Buchwald and Ruth Roston

White Flash / Black Rain:
Women of Japan Relive the Bomb
Edited and translated by Lequita Vance-Watkins
and Aratani Mariko

Milkweed Editions publishes with the intention of making a humane impact on society, in the belief that literature is a transformative art uniquely able to convey the essential experiences of the human heart and spirit.

To that end, Milkweed publishes distinctive voices of literary merit in handsomely designed, visually dynamic books, exploring the ethical, cultural, and esthetic issues that free societies need continually to address.

Milkweed Editions is a not-for-profit press.